WAR WITH NO END

WAR WITH NO END

Phyllis Bennis

Arundhati Roy

John Berger

Haifa Zangana

Hanif Kureishi

Joe Sacco

Ahdaf Soueif

Tram Nguyen

Naomi Klein

September 11th Families for Peaceful Tomorrows

VERSO

London • New York

First published by Verso 2007
© in the contributions to the individual contributors 2007
© in the collection Verso 2007
Reprinted with the author's permission: Arundhati Roy, "Come
September." First presented in Santa Fe, New Mexico at the Lensic
Performing Arts Center, 18 September 2002, sponsored by the
Lannan Foundation (www.lannan.org) and published in Arundhati
Roy, *War Talk* (Cambridge: South End Press 2004).
"Down! Up!" by Joe Sacco was first published by *Harpers Magazine*,
April 2007 issue. "Building A Booming Economy Based on War With
No End: The Lessons of Israel" by Naomi Klein is adapted from *The
Shock Doctrine: The Rise of Disaster Capitalism* (Harmondsworth:
Penguin 2007).

1 3 5 7 9 10 8 6 4 2

Verso
UK: 6 Meard Street, London W1F 0EG
USA: 180 Varick Street, New York, NY 10014-4606
www.versobooks.com

Verso is the imprint of New Left Books

ISBN-13: 978-1-84467-184-7

British Library Cataloguing in Publication Data
A catalogue record for this book is available from the British Library

Library of Congress Cataloging-in-Publication Data
A catalog record for this book
is available from the Library of Congress

Typeset in Sabon by Hewer Text UK Ltd, Edinburgh
"Printed in USA by Courier Stoughton Inc."
"Printed in UK by Bookmarque Limited, Croydon, Surrey"

Contents

JUDITH LE BLANC

United for Peace and Justice: A New Political Activism

Out of the extraordinary tragedy of September 11 2001, and the shameful events ensuing from that day, a new movement has arisen to challenge the Bush Administration. We have started to derail the neoconservatives' plan of war without end.

The anti-war movement in the US today is rooted amongst the poor and in working-class communities, in places of worship and in union halls. Veterans of past wars and soldiers returning from Iraq are marching alongside military families and those who have lost their loved ones to demand an end to the war and occupation in Iraq. Despite the Bush Administration's lies and manipulation of the mainstream media, an overwhelming majority of people today has come to believe that the war in Iraq was and continues to be a mistake that must end now. Getting to this point did not come easily.

Fear-mongering drove the politics of the US following September 11 2001, and the US peace and justice movement struggled to regain its footing in the wake of civil liberties being stripped away. Right wingers agitated furiously for the so-called "War on Terror", certain that this was the only possible response to a terrorist attack on US soil. On October 7 2001, the day on which the invasion of Afghanistan was initiated, thousands demonstrated for peace in New York.

Spearheaded by the National Youth and Student Peace Coalition, who collaborated with traditional peace organizations as well as Arab and Muslim communities, the peace and justice movement got back into the streets on April 20 2002, with nearly 100,000 turning out in Washington D.C. In October that year, 55 peace and justice groups gathered to launch a campaign to prevent a war on Iraq and founded a new national coalition, United For Peace and Justice (UFPJ). It was from the beginning a coalition whose aim was organizing mass action. At that time, the challenge was to shift the 45 percent of the public who believed that Saddam Hussein was hiding Weapons of Mass Destruction – and that military action was therefore necessary.

On February 15 2003, a "new superpower" (so named by the *New York Times*) came onto the scene worldwide. Tens of millions marched in cities around the world, including Manila, Auckland, Johannesburg and London. UFPJ organized a rally at the United Nations headquarters in New York City that drew more than 500,000 participants, along with another half a million who took part in over 400 smaller actions across the US, establishing itself as the representative of the majority who believed war was not the answer to the threat of terrorism.

A special relationship with our sister coalition, Stop the War UK, also began that day. Representatives of STW UK have spoken at almost every major UFPJ event and we at theirs. We each realize the urgent necessity of mutual support and solidarity. We both know that what the people of our countries do to end the war in Iraq makes a critical difference to people all over the world.

UFPJ has become the national umbrella of over 1,400 member groups. Our ranks include traditional peace and disarmament organizations as well as newer grassroots coalitions and groups. We have organized every major national action since before the war began, and we have nurtured grassroots activism and organization in every corner of the US. The coalition has continually linked the war in Iraq with the full spectrum of the Bush Administration's foreign policy. We have mobilized against the sabotage of peace efforts between Israel and Palestine, and joined the worldwide calls for an end to the Israeli occupation and prevention of preemptive strikes on Iran or North Korea.

UFPJ links the urgent struggles for justice here at home with the pressing need to end the war in Iraq. We have mobilized the anti-war movement to stand with immigrant communities and to speak out against budget cuts in human services and against corporate globalization.

The movements to end the war in Iraq, to uncover the lies and violations of civil rights and liberties, and in defense of democracy have given rise to a new political activism in the United States. This encompasses marching in the streets, participating in electoral battles, pressuring members of Congress, organizing neighborhood vigils or as simple an act as wearing tee shirts proclaiming outrage at the rich and powerful. It's a mass movement which grows stronger with each new revelation of the treachery of the Bush Administration.

On September 12 2001, no one could have predicted the growth of the massive opposition to the Bush administration's foreign and domestic policies. No one knew the depths of manipulation, lies and ruthlessness in the White House and its neoconservative advisers and supporters in the US Congress. Before the war began, 63 percent of the US people believed military action was necessary; 70 percent now want the troops to be withdrawn. The combination of the spiraling crisis in Iraq, the Bush administration's escalation of the war, and steadfast grassroots efforts across the US has shifted the political climate throughout the country.

When the war in Afghanistan was launched, the families who lost loved ones on September 11 popularized the slogan, "Our grief is not a cry for war." That sentiment is now more prevalent then ever. Where this mass outrage will be channeled is hard to predict. To put an end to the policy of the "War On Terror," political power must be shifted to the peaceful majority.

The world needs a US foreign policy premised on a commitment to international law and institutions, respect for national sovereignty and a willingness to participate in multilateral cooperation.

The "Bush Doctrine" of endless, preemptive war may be dying but there is a long road ahead before the wars in both Iraq and Afghanistan will be brought to an end; a longer road still for the damage to those countries to be repaired, lives reconstructed and communities rebuilt. Ending the war and occupation of Iraq is the leading edge of a movement that will continue to educate and mobilize grassroots opposition as the right wing scrambles to adjust to the new political terrain.

UFPJ is in the midst of a massive drive to turn opposition to the war into a political force that can compel the US Congress to end the war, rebuild Iraq and support the international efforts needed to enable the Iraqi people and their government to regain sovereignty.

In June 2007 UFPJ set as one of its top priorities the support of Iraq war veterans and their families in their acts of conscience to end this war. New efforts are underway to spread the movement for peace among active duty service members. The coalition is also launching a project to highlight the disparity between the billions of dollars spent on war and the 45 million Americans who have no healthcare insurance.

When we began to build the movement to prevent the war, we knew it would be a tough struggle. Over the past five years, we have succeeding in shifting public opinion and have been instrumental in creating a new moment of political activism. Now, we are organized in neighbor-hoods, workplaces, big cities and small rural towns. Now, the smoke has cleared and the overwhelming major-ity sees that the war on terror is a smokescreen for US military aggression.

Most citizens now realize that the bulk of the world's weapons of mass destruction have been in the US all along. They see that the invasion and occupation of Iraq had an agenda of corporate domination, war profiteering and control of oil.

Ending the wars in Afghanistan and Iraq was the catalyst for UFPJ but our mission has become far broader. With the lessons and successes of the past five years to grow from, we can go to the source. Our goal has evolved: We need to build a movement that will end the relentless right-wing drive for US military and economic global control.

The only way towards a peaceful and just world is to end the "War On Terror" and to put a stop to US foreign policy grounded in defending corporate interests and unilateralism. Our struggle is to replace it with a US foreign policy of peace and justice for the world and for the people at home. We have the momentum to do it – all we need is for you to join in!

Judith Le Blanc has been the National Co-chair of UFPJ for the past two years and has served on its national steering committee since its founding. She is American Indian, and a member of the Caddo Tribe of Oklahoma.

LINDSEY GERMAN

The Long War

The War On Terror has lasted longer than the First World War. Perhaps in recognition of this fact, George Bush's administration has renamed it the "long war." Far from winning its stated aim of ending terrorism and bringing democracy to countries invaded, bombed and occupied, terror attacks and organizations have grown. Democracy equates with pro-US governments in the occupied countries, while in countries such as Britain and the US there has been an assault on civil rights and freedoms in the name of combating "terrorism."

The human toll has been great and still rises. An estimated 655,000 Iraqi civilians had died as a result of the occupation up to autumn 2006. That is more than the total military and civilian casualties suffered by Britain during the Second World War from 1939–1945. Around 10,000 Afghans died during the bombardment and invasion of their country in 2001 and many thousands have died since. Such is the scale of civilian casualties in the country today, nearly six years after the war supposedly ended, that the pro-US president, Hamid Karzai, has been forced repeatedly to criticize the tactics of the Nato forces. Over 150 British soldiers have been killed in Iraq, and more than 60 in Afghanistan. The US military toll in Iraq is much higher, with over 3,500 dead.

Those lucky enough to survive do not escape the consequences of war. One grim statistic, rarely commented on in the Western media, comes from the UNHCR: around 4 million Iraqis are refugees, half of them within their country's borders, half of them in other countries.

We should remember this whenever we hear politicians claim that invading Iraq was the right thing to do, or that we have to stay to finish the job, or that Iraqis' lives would have been worse without the invasion. Our governments have presided over one of the greatest man-made disasters of modern times, whose consequences they would prefer to forget.

Indeed, the logic of colonial occupation (for that is what it is) spurs them on to greater disaster. The US and its allies are now intervening (directly), by direct occupation or by arming and funding one side against the other, in six predominantly Muslim countries: Iraq, Afghanistan, Palestine, Lebanon, Somalia and Sudan. Their economic and military might allows them to bribe, bully, and coerce many more, including most of the dictatorships and autocratic monarchies of the region.

The same advocates of neo-liberalism who preach privatization at home want to enforce these policies with bombs and guns abroad. The new imperialism is the means by which the poorest countries are brought into line, their rulers allowed a space at the big powers' table as long as they agree to take the medicine first, however unpalatable it may be.

There were many lies and deceptions which took us into war: the staggering double standards which brought war in the name of women's rights to Afghanistan but left Saudi Arabia a close ally of the West; the contempt for so many, from the Pope to Nelson Mandela to the millions who marched around the world.

It is important to mark why the war has been such a

political mistake for its main architects, Bush and Blair (and their friends Aznar and Berlusconi), and why it continues to dominate politics in the US and Britain more than four years after George Bush landed on the decks of the aircraft carrier USS *Vincennes* and declared peace against a banner reading "mission accomplished."

The main reason for that can be summed up in the word "resistance": millions of people around the world opposed the war from the start and continue to oppose it. From day one of the occupation, Iraqis fought against the occupiers while mass popular opinion across the world remained skeptical about the war. Huge mobilizations have dogged George Bush wherever he goes. All of that has forced the issue onto the political agenda and has made it impossible for the imperialist powers to win.

Resistance continues with those who refuse to abandon demonstrating outside parliament, with the Military Families against the War who have lost loved ones and now campaign against the war, and in the growing expression of anti-war sentiment amongst those involved in music, art, theater, poetry, and the writings contained in this collection. All are testimony to a mass movement which, although it did not stop the war, informed, organized and radicalized millions of people.

The war in Lebanon in summer 2006 – seen by many as a war of aggression against Lebanon by Israel – marked another turning point. International public opinion was horrified at Bush and Blair's refusal to even call for a ceasefire. In Britain two major demonstrations were followed by political pressure on Blair to name a date for his resignation, which he duly did an estimated two years before he had planned to leave office. Bush has become even more of a lame duck President, fatally wounded in the November 2006 mid-term Congressional elections.

Now we face a new challenge for the movement. Blair has gone, Bush will soon follow him, yet the legacy of the "War On Terror" remains. The deadly game of consequences they started continues to affect new areas and create new political problems. There is hope (from some quarters) that new government will mean change of policy. Certainly the Brown government is trying to distance itself from Blair on this issue, but as yet there is no sign of a change in policy. The Americans have never needed British troops militarily in Iraq, but they are politically vital to continuing the pretence of a coalition.

Brown has bankrolled these wars, has never spoken out against them, and seems unlikely to break with the US President on this issue. The movement therefore has to continue and grow, calling for a change in foreign policy to include the immediate withdrawal of troops and no further support for US military action against other countries.

The future of humanity depends on this change: we can either fall deeper into barbarism, or we can build a world where peace, justice, and equality are the guiding principles of relations between countries. This issue remains paramount in Britain, alongside the defense of civil liberties and opposition to racism against the Muslim community. Any government which wages war against the wishes of the majority has to try to marginalize or criminalize those who protest against it. Protests are banned in the name of security, surveillance is increased. The Muslim community, strongly opposed to the war, now finds itself subject to equation with extremism and even terrorism. Calls to integrate by politicians, stop and search by police, and attacks by the racist right are all consequences of the government's attempt to evade responsibility for its disastrous foreign policy.

The Stop the War Coalition is the largest mass movement ever seen in Britain and has now sustained itself over six years. It has been a genuinely integrated and diverse movement, involving those of all religions and none, old, young, gay, straight, female and male. It has affiliates in all the main trade unions, support from many Muslim organizations, and has thousands of supporters around Britain. With threats of a further escalation of war to Iran, with the troops still in Iraq and Afghanistan, we are going to continue to be active. We have no choice.

PHYLLIS BENNIS

The Global War On Terror: What It Is, What It's Done to the World

Six years after the September 11 attacks, six years after the war against Afghanistan began, six years after the proudly sanctioned shredding of Americans' civil liberties went into high gear, six years after the politics of fear seized control of US national life. Where are we now?

Some things are all too easy to identify. The illegal US-British invasion and ensuing occupation of Iraq, now well into its fifth year, continues to spawn death and destruction on an almost incomprehensible scale. Israel's US-enabled occupation of Palestine rises to new crisis points almost daily, escalating the political and humanitarian catastrophe, and creating dangerous regional and global consequences. Threats of a reckless US military strike against Iran remain on the table of Washington's powerful. The US continues to shower money, arms and diplomatic protection on repressive regimes from Uzbekistan to Colombia to Pakistan, embracing them as close allies in the global war on terror.

So what is this "Global War On Terror" that has gone so far in reshaping our world? While Washington's "GWOT" acronym appropriately hints at an unnerving evil, this carefully crafted framework is not simply a propaganda device. Like its predecessor, the cold war, the GWOT plays two roles simultaneously. On the one hand, it is an ideological framework designed to legitimize the US "right" to military, economic, political and cultural domination.

And at the same time, however false the notion of actually waging a "war on terror," the Global War On Terror is also an actual war – not a war on terror but a worldwide war waged for power and control of resources. It is a real war that kills real people, destroys real countries and devastates real societies. To push the parallel even further, just as the cold war identified its enemy of choice, communism, the global war on terror has targeted its own enemy "other" – political Islam.

Despite repetitive claims of top Bush and Blair administration officials that "Islam is a religion of peace," "Islam is not our enemy," and various versions of "some of my best friends are Muslims," there is no doubt that political Islam, and its ostensible terrorist core, has become the over-arching adversary for US- and UK-backed wars and threats of wars across the Muslim world. Through sophisticated demonization campaigns, repressive but thoroughly secular Muslim leaders like Saddam Hussein become linked in the public mind with Islamist fundamentalists like Osama bin Laden. Islamic nationalist organizations like Hamas or Hezbollah and some Iraqi Islamist parties, which have expanded from social service/political movements (albeit with military wings) to become popular parliamentary parties contending for state power and legitimized in internationally sanctioned elections, are equated with extreme fundamentalist anti-state forces like al Qaeda and its now-numerous offshoots.

It should be noted that these Islamic nationalist forces, using Islam as a political framework to shape anti-occupation movements, were all created or expanded under conditions of military occupation. Hezbollah was born in South Lebanon in response to the 1982 Israeli invasion and occupation, when the Israeli-backed government in Beirut had largely abandoned the social needs of the people of the South. In the Israeli-occupied Gaza Strip in 1987, Hamas emerged first as an Islamic-flavored but largely social welfare-focused organization, providing health clinics, summer camps and other social needs for the impoverished population – and was allowed to thrive because Israel hoped it would challenge the more popular secular nationalism of the PLO. And in Iraq, despite their longer underground history, the powerful Islamist parties won wide popular support only after US and British troops had occupied their country in 2003.

After the attacks of September 11 2001, ruling forces in Washington immediately moved to shape a new global strategy targeting the new enemy – an enemy combining the two powerful symbols of the 9/11 attack, Islam and terrorism. It is telling how the reality of those terrorist attacks was so quickly seized and twisted by those in the US already seeking new ways to legitimize US militarism and unilateralism. The attacks of September 11 2001 were not the only attacks in the world (not even the only attacks on September 11 – on that day in 1973 the US-backed Chilean General Augusto Pinochet overthrew the democratically elected government of Salvador Allende, leading to the murder of over 3000 people, and the arrest and torture of tens of thousands more). Certainly for the people of the US the 2001 attacks were shocking – not least because they violated a century-old sense of impunity, the widespread view that the US homeland and population were somehow invulnerable from any consequences of its government's foreign policies, that the combination of size, geography and oceans, and sheer power made such an attack impossible. That shock set the stage for the politics of fear, and the success of Washington's new reliance on "anti-terrorism" to justify a new "war."

The US was not the first country whose people were victims of a cruel terror attack – an attack more properly identified as a crime against humanity. But only in the US was a terror attack answered not by a call for justice but by a declaration of war. In the rest of the world, reactions to terrorist attacks – the Madrid train bombings, the 2005 British subway attacks and the more recent attempted car bombings there, the nightclub attacks in Bali – remain very different. As one analyst noted in the Saudi *Arab News* immediately after the summer 2007 UK events:

> European countries had already been through some sort of terrorist crisis well before the current fashion for "Islamist" terrorism: The IRA in Britain, the OAS in France, ETA in Spain, the Baader-Meinhof Gang in Germany, the Brigate Rossi and their neofascist counterparts in Italy.
>
> Most European cities have also been heavily bombed in a real war within living memory, which definitely puts terrorist attacks into a less impressive category. So most Europeans, while they dislike terrorist attacks, do not obsess about them: They know that they are likelier to win the lottery than to be hurt by terrorists.
>
> Russians are pretty cool about the occasional terrorist attacks linked to the war in Chechnya, and Indians are positively heroic in their refusal (most of the time) to be panicked by terrorist attacks that have taken more lives there than all the attacks in the West since terrorist techniques first became widespread in the 1960s.
>
> In almost all of these countries, despite the efforts of some governments to convince the population that terrorism is an existential threat of enormous size, the vast majority of the people don't believe it.
>
> Whereas in the United States, most people do believe it.[1]

THE NEW EMPIRE

What quickly became clear was that the wars that were to follow September 11 in such quick succession – Afghanistan, Iraq, Lebanon/Gaza – and the alliances that were to be created or strengthened, with Pakistan, Uzbekistan, Saudi Arabia and other repressive dictatorships, had little to do with Islam or even Islamic nationalist resistance movements. What the newly created "enemy" provided was a new way to justify expanding the longstanding US drive for power and control of resources.

Addressing the glitterati of the annual World Economic Forum in Davos, 2004, Vice-President Cheney said that "if we were a true empire, we would currently preside over a much greater piece of the earth's surface than we do. That's not the way we operate."[2]

In fact, he was right. What is now commonly described as a US drive for "empire" looks quite different from empires of old. Seizing land and settling colonists on others' territory defined earlier versions of colonialism and imperialism. During the Cold War control of land had already begun to shift from direct control by the empire's own armies and settlers to a new "neo-colonial" version in which the US backed local surrogate forces to hold the land and guarantee US access to resources. "Vietnamization" was only the most explicitly named version; the Carter Doctrine would combine political and military control of local governments with the expansion of US troop deployments to defend US control of, among other things, "our oil" that just happened to be under the sands of the Persian Gulf. Control of resources and expansion of power through a global network of military bases would define the twenty-first century US empire.

Afghanistan had been the site of a hoped-for oil pipeline since the 1980s. During the brutal war between US-backed and other Afghan factions, Washington's current UN ambassador Zalmay Khalilzad was a UNOCAL consultant who brought the Taliban's oil chiefs to Texas to negotiate a deal. Not secretly – there were articles in major magazines at the time. But somehow it wasn't known; and of course it never came up in Khalilzad's confirmation hearings as ambassador to Iraq and then the UN. Just weeks after the September 11 attacks, analyst Michael Klare wrote that:

> Osama bin Laden does not talk about oil when he calls for a holy war against the enemies of Islam. Neither does George Bush when he calls for a global war against terrorism. Both major protagonists in the current conflict stress moral and religious themes in their public pronouncements, claiming that this is a struggle between good and evil. But both bin Laden and Bush are well aware that the conflict also represents a struggle for control over the greater Persian Gulf region – the location of about two-thirds of the world's known petroleum reserves . . . [I]t is not possible to fully appreciate the origins and significance of the conflict without considering the historic role of oil politics.[3]

It was not only oil, of course. Uzbekistan isn't known for its oil riches – but the establishment of US military bases on its territory conveniently close not only to Afghanistan but to several transnational oil and gas pipelines in the region, certainly made it worth Washington's while to abandon even the pretext of concern about Uzbekistan's dictatorship. The expansion of US military bases around the world – today there are more than 700 – has been an important tactic that both predates and follows the announcement of the Global War On Terror. (It is telling that the Pentagon's "Base Structure Report – as of 30 September 2005" documenting the existence and construction of military bases and installations around the world – these totaled 702 in 2006 – does NOT include those bases in countries most central to the so-called Global War On Terror. It simply excludes any reference to bases in Iraq, Afghanistan, Uzbekistan, Oman, Qatar and more.)

When the attacks of September 11 came along, the process of establishing bases in formerly off-limits areas moved into high gear. Grudging respect for post-Soviet Russia's "sphere of influence" in the former Soviet republics had prevented major US efforts to expand its network of bases into places like Tajikistan, Uzbekistan and elsewhere. And human rights violations of the most egregious kind had made it rather embarrassing for US officials to embrace some of these governments. But, as the British *Guardian* noted in 2003 regarding Uzbekistan, "the government of President Islam Karimov has become Washington's new best friend in the region. The US is funding those it once condemned. Last year Washington gave Uzbekistan $500m (£300m) in aid. The police and intelligence services – which the State Department's website says use 'torture as a routine investigation technique' received $79m of this sum." According to British embassy forensic reports, that torture included two victims who were boiled to death.[4] A US base in Uzbekistan was indeed built, and used for flights into adjacent Afghanistan until the Uzbek government closed it down in 2005.

That new impunity for US allies in the Global War On Terror also included support for military dictatorships. Pakistan's coup-installed president, General Pervez Musharraf, was given a pass when he ignored his own claimed commitment to democratic elections. And Washington quickly ended the mild sanctions it had imposed after Pakistan's 1998 explosion of a nuclear bomb. In return, the Musharraf government granted free access to US special operations and other military forces to its entire strategic border zone with Afghanistan. The US empire was expanding, and the Global War On Terror was providing the excuse.

And this was all before the war in Iraq even began.

BEFORE

Virtually all of the US assertions of militarism and unilateralism that followed the September 11 attacks have their roots in earlier US crusades for global power and control of resources. When the planes hit the World Trade Center and the Pentagon on September 11, the Bush administration responded by heading into what European security chief Chris Patten would later call "unilateralist overdrive."[5] Within twenty-four hours, President Bush announced that the attacks were "more than acts of terror. They were acts of war." Not just any war, he told reporters assembled in the White House Cabinet Room, but a war that "will be a monumental struggle between good and evil. But good will prevail." To carry out that war, Bush said, he would rally the world.[6]

The war would be waged against "evil." But evil doesn't have a face, a name, a bomb-reachable address. Islamic fundamentalism, or Islamic radicals, or Muslims linked to terrorists – they had it all: Osama bin Laden was the name and face, Afghanistan the all-too-bombable address. At first the face was only that of bin Laden, the charismatic, wealthy Saudi financier, onetime client of the CIA and other US agencies fighting Soviet forces in Afghanistan throughout the 1980s, and soon found to be at the center of the movement responsible for September 11 – later Saddam Hussein would take his place as the target. The campaign of demonization began quickly. But despite bin Laden's years of alliances with the US, there was no need to create this campaign out of thin air; there was a long history to fall back on.

The demonization of a former Arab ally had been crafted quite brilliantly in 1990, when Saddam Hussein, long one of Washington's favorite Middle East dictators, ordered his military to invade Kuwait, whose emir was somewhat higher on the favored Arab dictator list. To erase the longstanding US backing of Saddam Hussein (Washington had provided Iraq with arms, funds, satellite targeting information for chemical weapons attacks, even seed stock for the much-hyped biological weapons programs), a massive campaign was launched to equate the Iraqi leader with Hitler, with pure evil. The wire service photo of the warm 1983 handshake between Saddam Hussein and Donald Rumsfeld somehow disappeared from public view (the internet wasn't yet omnipresent). The demonization was powerful enough that for the first half of a dozen years of crippling US-led economic sanctions, opposition was muted because so many Americans believed Iraq was populated by 20 million Saddam Husseins.

The technique, of course, did not start even with Saddam Hussein. More than a decade earlier, when the US-backed Shah of Iran was overthrown by a popular revolution whose leader declared Iran to be an Islamic republic, the image of the Ayatollah Ruhollah Khomeini quickly spread from "target" style T-shirts to racist dolls and more. By the time pro-Khomeini students in Tehran engineered the hostage-taking of the US embassy staff, outrage at all things Iranian spiked sky-high.

And indeed shortly after 9/11 it became clear that despite the initial focus on bin Laden and the Taliban, the old favorite target Saddam Hussein remained at the top of the demonization list. War on Afghanistan was the immediate goal, justified as self-defense despite the fact that neither the government nor the people of Afghanistan had actually attacked the US on 9/11. But Iraq was clearly the more strategic target, right from the beginning.

This was not a war on "evil." This would be a war for control of strategic resources – Iraq and Iran both had long been countries the US was determined to influence or control. Certainly, like Saudi Arabia and others in the region, they have large amounts of oil. But there is more to it – of all the countries of the Middle East, only Iran and Iraq had all the requirements to become indigenous regional powers – which could someday challenge the global hegemon operating in their neighborhood. Those requisites are water, oil for wealth, and large size of land and population – and no other Middle Eastern country has all three. (Of course since the devastation wrought by the US-British invasion and occupation, Iraq hardly qualifies as an indigenous power at all.)

And further, perhaps not coincidentally, Iran and Iraq were among the very few Middle Eastern countries (Egypt being the other exception) with their own history as nation-states. Unlike the majority of Arab countries, created in 1922 when British and French colonial officials drew lines on a map to create Saudi Arabia, Jordan, Oman, Qatar, Kuwait, etc., Iraq's history (with only slightly different borders) as ancient Mesopotamia and Iran's similar legacy as the center of the Persian empires gave rise to far stronger national identities than in any of the surrounding countries.

In January 2002 Bush announced that US military capacity would be built up to wage his new war, "whatever it takes, whatever it costs."[7] But in fact the strategic gap between the U.S and the rest of the world, that became apparent in the response to 9/11, was so vast that no immediate emergency spending alone could have created it was already underway. The $48 billion addition to the Pentagon budget requested by the Bush administration in January 2002 by itself was more money than any other country spent on its military – and that was on top of the existing $379 billion military budget.[8] In US terms alone, the Global War On Terror's budget included by far the biggest defense increase since the Cold War.[9]

What emerged from September 11 was the largest, most powerful mobilization of US forces – military as well as political – in history. It set in motion what the influential editor of *Newsweek International*, Fareed Zakaria, called "a new era of American hegemony."[10] It was a thoroughly militarized unilateralism, one that legitimized, even glorified, the use of US military force anywhere in the world, with the unchallengeable expectation that the world would join the crusade. It demonstrated quickly that while Washington's rhetoric identified September 11 as an attack on the whole [at least civilized] world, the US had no need for the rest of the world to agree to the nature of its response.

The world's leaders, the world's governments, did not immediately object. To the contrary. Before September 11, anti-Bush outrage was already rising among French intellectuals watching the US hyper-power behaving like an empire. Before September 11, Russia was audibly objecting to US threats to abandon the ABM treaty. Before September 11, Europeans and others had begun cautious efforts to punish Washington's lack of accountability to the international community, through such moves as stripping the US of its seat on the UN Human Rights Commission. But by 9 a.m. on that September Tuesday, all those already hesitant moves came to an abrupt stop.

Instead, for a while, governments cheered and much of the world stood by as the US asserted the rights of empire. "Nous sommes tous les Américains," proclaimed *Le*

Monde's September 13 headline in Paris. We are all Americans.

Public support in the US for the ever-expanding Global War On Terror – limitless, borderless war on Afghanistan, then Iraq, and perhaps beyond – was rooted in fear. This instrumentalizing of fear gave the Bush administration enormous power, as individuals across the US suddenly responded to the sense of individual vulnerability that accompanied the loss of national impunity after September 11. It was in that context that anti-terrorism – the GWOT – took hold as the new justification for US foreign policy. This framework not only supplanted the anti-communism of the Cold War and George Bush Senior's New World Order, it also quickly laid to rest the global interventionism masquerading as multilateralism that lay at the heart of the Clinton foreign policy.

Press accounts reported that as early as the evening of September 11 Bush had already decided to respond to the attacks with war, and told his advisers that he saw the attacks as an opportunity. It was consistent with his administration's pre-9/11 positions; even before his administration had come to power, Bush's soon-to-be-appointed Secretary of Defense Donald Rumsfeld told the president he believed that US military power was needed "to help discipline the world."[11]

That "discipline" would come in two ways. Internationally, the US would use its newly-claimed victim status to justify a strategy based on asserting the right of unilateral military power. Bush would claim that right by distorting the careful, limited self-defense language of the UN Charter's Article 51, to a new definition allowing the US to wage an infinitely expandable, unilaterally determined, borderless, limitless war. No United Nations approval would be sought, because that would imply recognition of the global organization's authority (in fact mandated in the UN Charter, the linchpin of international law) to determine such legitimacy or lack thereof. Instead, an international "coalition" would be bribed and coerced into being, first for expanding US military and bases around the world and later to wage war on Iraq. There was no illusion that the coalition's member governments held decision-making power; the coalition's role was to bolster and justify US strategic decisions, not to participate in making them.

There was a rush to join the US crusade – even before it was clear just what it was that they were joining. By mid-2002, before the Iraq "coalition of the willing" was officially announced, seventy-six governments had granted landing rights in their countries for US military operations. Twenty-three governments offered bases for US forces involved in offensive operations of the GWOT. When the invasion of Iraq began in 2003, the US claimed there were about thirty-four governments supporting the US (although the US refused to name some, respecting governments' fear of wide-spread domestic opposition). By February 2007, there were less than 14,200 "coalition" troops in Iraq, and only two countries (Britain and South Korea) had more than 1000 troops there. Of the other nineteen countries in the "coalition" by that time, seven had fewer than 100 troops in Iraq.[12]

Since 9/11 we have seen the GWOT framework used to justify a wide range of military attacks. In Somalia, the US backed an Ethiopian invasion described as necessary to prevent the Islamic Courts Movement government from establishing its tentative stability in Mogadishu, followed by direct US bombing in January 2007. GWOT-related involvement in Africa includes plans to create the Pentagon's newest regional force, the Africa Command or Afri-Com, which will continue to distort the economies of the region in favor of militarization, as well as bringing all aspects of already meager US assistance – economic aid, development assistance, HIV/AIDS support, food and humanitarian aid, etc. – under the control of the Pentagon. The GWOT fails to mandate real support for the African Union/United Nations effort to stop the crisis in Darfur, and the effort to maintain US control of Nigerian oil gains strength as US oil sources in the Middle East and elsewhere are threatened by GWOT-driven wars.

At home, the president's discipline was imposed on the rest of government by consolidating the power of the executive branch, against the virtual exclusion from power of the legislative and judicial branches of government. Congress was granted the barest modicum of collaboration. And the American people were "disciplined" with a systematic stripping away of the Constitutional protections and civil liberties that had once been the claimed hallmark of the American system of government.

Globally, the effort to impose discipline on an unruly world has come to be known as the Bush Doctrine – expressed in the president's Wild West-style threat that "you're either with us, or with the terrorists." Governments around the world scrambled to remake their image in official American eyes, repressive regimes held publicly at arms length by a virtuous State Department transforming themselves overnight to vigorous allies clamping down on opposition movements. If their separatist or nationalist opponents could be demonized as Islamist-oriented, they gained extra points. If they suddenly "discovered" their opposition movements to be home-grown versions of al-Qaeda terrorists, even better – and they would have a good shot at a White House photo-op. In the Philippines, for example, the violent but tiny Abu Sayyaf gang of criminal thugs on one southern island was upgraded by Pentagon fiat (quickly parroted by much of the US media as well as the US-oriented Philippine government) to new status as the suddenly-discovered Southeast Asian branch of al-Qaeda. The Global War On Terror now shaped Washington's new public acceptance of what had once been – however self-righteously – condemned as human rights violations.

GWOT IN IRAQ

Then came the Iraq war. Contemplated almost from the moment of the September 11 attacks, the early justifications for the White House's long-desired war reflected the public relations success of the GWOT framework. Relying on fear, the looming war against Iraq was shaped as the necessary answer to Iraqi weapons of mass destruction, the build up of Iraq's nuclear weapons programs, the ties between Saddam Hussein and Osama bin Laden as well as between Iraq and al-Qaeda, and concomitant responsibility of Iraq for the September 11 attacks . . . none of which, of course, existed. Only after the invasion, and only after the war's brutality was revealed in the rising levels of death and destruction in occupied Iraq, was the replacement pretext – democratization – brought to center stage to justify the clearly unjustifiable war.

The war against Iraq – beginning months before it began – generated the largest, broadest, most truly international anti-war mobilization of any war in the history of humanity, linking popular movements, governments, and ultimately the United Nations. Surpassing even the massive protests against the Viet Nam war, the February 15, 2003 demonstrations in which "The World Says No to War" brought out between 12 and 14 million people in the streets of 665 cities around the world. According to the 2004 Guinness Book of Records, it was the largest mass protest in human history.

In the US and the UK, the centerpieces of the Iraq invasion and occupation, United for Peace and Justice and the Stop the War Coalition led the rising resistance. But quickly, again even before the war began, pressures on the streets of their own capitals began pushing governments around the world to turn away from the "coalition of the coerced" to join the new internationalist challenge to the Bush-led drive towards empire. The biggest protests took to the streets in countries whose governments were supporting the war, against massive public opposition: 1.3 million in Barcelona, a million in London, almost two million in Rome. Even in Bulgaria, hardly a hotbed of protest, demonstrators came out with signs calling on their government to "Send Weapons Inspectors to US."

Eventually, the war's wealthy powerful opponents in the Security Council, Germany, Russia and France, were joined by what came to be known as the "Uncommitted Six" – the largely poor, relatively weak countries who under ordinary circumstances would never risk going head to head with the US. But these were no ordinary circumstances. The growing antiwar pressures – from the public and from other governments – set the stage for Guinea, Cameroon, Angola, Pakistan, Chile and Mexico all to resist intense US pressure to give in and endorse Washington's war.

The intimidation was powerful: Guinea and Cameroon were threatened with losing the tiny amounts of aid they receive under the Africa Growth and Opportunities Act (AGOA), which stipulated that no country receiving aid under that act could do anything that might undermine [unspecified] US foreign policy interests. Chile, whose government had just completed seven strenuous years of negotiating a free trade agreement with Washington, was warned that the treaty would never be brought for ratification if they did not sign on. Mexico was told that a refusal to join the US-UK crusade would mean an end to any further negotiations over the US-Mexico border issues.

But not one of the countries gave in. And the global movement – remaining in the streets, occupying the capitals, keeping up the pressure on their own governments and parliaments as well as on the embassies and missions of other countries, persisted[kept up the pressure]. Soon public mobilizations targeted the United Nations itself, focusing on the Security Council where protesters encouraged the resisting governments to hold fast, and loudly demanded that the US and its allies back down.

It is significant that of all the dire threats Washington made against resisting governments, not one was implemented. Guinea and Cameroon did not lose their AGOA aid; Chile got its free trade agreement, and Mexico continued border negotiations. In fact just months later, when the World Trade Organization met in Cancun, the model of Security Council resistance probably played a part in the decision of scores of countries of the Global South to refuse to give in to US-European pressure on crucial trade issues. After all, their representatives likely thought, they got away with it at the UN, why not at the WTO? The Cancun summit thoroughly derailed the planned expansion of WTO power.

On February 15, when most of the world's cities' protests had already ended, one of the last was just beginning. In New York City, just blocks from the United Nations, half a million people braved bitter winds to hear activists, religious and political leaders, artists and politicians link their work to that of the global mobilization. Mid-way through that rally, a brief story broke on the Associated Press wire, relayed backstage by cellphone and quickly announced to the massive crowd. It said "rattled by an outpouring of international anti-war sentiment, the

United States and Britain began reworking a draft resolution Saturday to authorize force against Saddam Hussein. Diplomats, speaking on condition of anonymity, said the final product may be a softer text that does not explicitly call for war."

It meant that whatever their real plans – and they would invade Iraq less than a month later – Washington and London realized they would not have international legitimacy when they did it. The movement had triumphed. Not surprisingly, it was only a day later that the *New York Times* recognized on its front page that there were "once again two superpowers in the world. The United States, and global public opinion."[13]

GWOT IN PALESTINE

The framework of the Global War On Terror, which took hot war form first in Afghanistan, then in Iraq, was also playing out in occupied Palestinian territory. The first large-scale national US protest against the war in Afghanistan, held in April 2002, happened to match the timing of Israel's military reoccupation of the West Bank's cities. The resulting massacre and humanitarian crisis, especially in the city and refugee camp of Jenin in the northern West Bank, put the issue of Palestine and the longstanding US support for Israeli occupation squarely on the agenda of the anti-war movement, which had for many years resisted confronting it directly.

During the early stages of the post-9/11 assertion of the GWOT, the Bush administration had vacillated on how it would implement its support for Israel. During the first months of Bush's presidency, his administration had appeared to distance itself slightly from Israel, focusing its Middle East policy more specifically on supporting the oil-rich Arab regimes and the search for regional stability. But within hours of the 9/11 attacks, Israeli leaders and pro-Israeli officials and analysts across the United States realized the potential value of linking support for Israel with the new "war on – Islamic – terrorism." Writing only hours after the World Trade Center was attacked, *New York Time* columnist Clyde Haberman weighed in, asking "do you get it now? It is a question that many Israelis wanted to ask yesterday of America and the rest of the finger-pointing world. Not in a smart-alecky manner. Not to say, 'We told you so.' . . . It was simply a question for those who, at a safe remove from the terrorism that Israelis face every day, have damned Israel for taking admittedly harsh measures to keep its citizens alive."[14]

How convenient, as the GWOT framework took shape, to have a close ally eager to join in grasping and legitimizing the "admittedly harsh measures" that lay ahead.

Opposition to the Israeli occupation has continued to rise globally and more and more people are using the framework of Apartheid to explain Israeli policy towards Palestinians, but simultaneously the occupation itself has pushed further. In the occupied Palestinian territory Israel is stealing more Palestinian land, building the Apartheid Wall deemed illegal by the International Court of Justice, turning Gaza into a prison territory despite the claims of "disengagement," and violating international law and UN resolutions with the impunity of uncritical US support. And following the February 2006 election that brought Hamas to legitimate power in the Palestinian Authority legislature, the US-Israeli led boycott that brought about such humanitarian crises for Palestinians was justified through invoking the specter of terrorism once again. Even the much-heralded Bush administration infatuation with the forms of electoral democracy was not enough to overcome the anti-Hamas mobilization in the context of the GWOT.

In the years since, the broad anti-war movement has moved dramatically in linking the struggle against the Iraq war with campaigns against US support for Israeli occupation and violations of international law. In the US, where the linkage was historically more difficult, the growing collaboration between United for Peace and Justice and the US Campaign to End Israeli Occupation made possible a strengthening of both issues through a "dual occupations" framework. Both movements have been strengthened as a result.

Another aspect of the GWOT, however, has got decreasing attention over time – that is the first of the set of wars, the one in Afghanistan. Early justifications, including the claim that "we are invading Afghanistan to liberate its women" and the "one US-sanctioned election equals democracy" appropriately failed. The fundamental basis of the Afghanistan war, however, is not rooted in elections or women's rights – it was launched to provide a post-9/11 "self-defense" argument that would set the stage for later wars, and the Bush administration commitment to "regime change" wherever they can overthrow an Islamist regime. As a result, there are high levels of ambivalence, and even outright support for the US/NATO occupation of Afghanistan despite the escalating levels of civilian casualties. The failure to keep the Afghanistan war on top of the anti-war agenda in the US has helped create a scenario in which many elite liberal forces, including top officials of the Democratic Party, shape their ostensible opposition to the Iraq war in the context of needing to "address the real war against terrorism in Afghanistan."

BUILDING A GLOBAL MOVEMENT

As the anti-war movements of the US and the UK move forward, it must be in the context of participation in a broad global movement. Work in electoral campaigns will often be crucially important, but the need to maintain independent social movements which will stand by their principles and reject the compromises endemic to party leaders and candidates, cannot be overstated. Our movements must continue to recognize that the Global War On Terror is not only a convenient ideological frame, but a real set of wars and potential wars, capable of destroying the lives of millions.

Especially in the US, people around the world look to us not only as part of the global movement, but as the part that must play the central role in challenging the US drive towards empire. And that means keeping our primacy on the work inside the US. However important our involvement with the global anti-bases coalition, with the World Social Forum process, with projects like the Jakarta Peace Consensus or the Italian campaign to stop the new US base in Vicenza – and it IS important – our collective priority must remain building a powerful enough campaign inside the US that the work of all those global movements will make our broad collective goals possible. We will work to end the occupation of Iraq and bring all the troops and mercenaries home, to close the US bases and stop trying to control Iraqi oil. We will work to end US support for Israeli apartheid and occupation, to prevent any US or allied military strike on Iran, and to finally end the US drive towards war and empire. And we will work to replace it with an entirely new foreign policy based not on expanding power and controlling resources, but on international law, equality, human rights, and justice.

NOTES

1. Gwynne Dyer, "Why Europe Reacts to Terrorism in a Different Way", *Arab News*, July 1 2007.
2. By Arlene Getz, " 'We Must Work Together': Dick Cheney tried to strike a conciliatory note in Davos. Not Everyone Was Convinced", *Newsweek,* January 24 2005.
3. Michael T. Klare, "What bin Laden and Bush Don't Talk About: The Politics of Oil", Alternet, November 5 2001.
4. Nick Paton, "US looks away as new ally tortures Islamists", *The Guardian*, May 26 2003.
5. National Public Radio, March 1 2002.
6. Bob Woodward and Dan Balz, " 'We Will Rally the World' ", *Washington Post*, January 28 2002.
7. President George Bush, CNN, January 23 2002.
8. "Proposed Pentagon Budget Hike More Than Other Countries' Military Spending", AP, January 26 2002.
9. "Terror Prompts Huge U.S. Military Revamp", BBC, February 1 2002.
10. Lehrer News Hour, March 11 2002.
11. Woodward and Balz, op cit.
12. Global Security, "Iraq Coalition Troops: Non-US Forces in Iraq – February 2007", http://www.globalsecurity.org/military/ops/iraq_orbat_coalition.htm.
13. Patrick E. Tyler, "A New Power in the Streets", *New York Times*, February 17 2003.
14. Clyde Haberman, "When the Unimaginable Happens, and It's Right Outside Your Window", *New York Times*, September 12 2001.

ARUNDHATI ROY

Come September

Writers imagine that they cull stories from the world. I'm beginning to believe that vanity makes them think so. That it's actually the other way around. Stories cull writers from the world. Stories reveal themselves to us. The public narrative, the private narrative – they colonize us. They commission us. They insist on being told. Fiction and non-fiction are only different techniques of story telling. For reasons I do not fully understand, fiction dances out of me. Non-fiction is wrenched out by the aching, broken world I wake up to every morning.

The theme of much of what I write, fiction as well as non-fiction, is the relationship between power and powerlessness and the endless, circular conflict they're engaged in. John Berger, that most wonderful writer, once wrote: Never again will a single story be told as though it's the only one. There can never be a single story. There are only ways of seeing.[1] So when I tell a story, I tell it not as an ideologue who wants to pit one absolutist ideology against another, but as a story-teller who wants to share her way of seeing. Though it might appear otherwise, my writing is not really about nations and histories, it's about power. About the paranoia and ruthlessness of power. About the physics of power. I believe that the accumulation of vast unfettered power by a state or a country, a corporation or an institution – or even an individual, a spouse, friend or sibling – regardless of ideology, results in excesses such as the ones I will recount here.

Living as I do, as millions of us do, in the shadow of the nuclear holocaust that the governments of India and Pakistan keep promising their brainwashed citizenry, and in the global neighborhood of the War On Terror (what President Bush rather biblically calls "The Task That Does Not End"), I find myself thinking a great deal about the relationship between Citizens and the State.[2]

In India, those of us who have expressed views on Nuclear Bombs, Big Dams, Corporate Globalization and the rising threat of communal Hindu fascism – views that are at variance with the Indian Government's – are branded "anti-national." While this accusation does not fill me with indignation, it's not an accurate description of what I do or how I think. An "anti-national" is a person is who is against his/her own nation and, by inference, is pro some other one. But it isn't necessary to be "anti-national" to be deeply suspicious of all nationalism, to be anti-national*ism*. Nationalism of one kind or another was the cause of most of the genocide of the twentieth century. Flags are bits of colored cloth that governments use first to shrink-wrap people's minds and then as ceremonial shrouds to bury the dead. When independent, thinking people (and here I do not include the corporate media) begin to rally under flags, when writers, painters, musicians, film makers suspend their judgment and blindly yoke their art to the service of the "Nation," it's time for all of us to sit up and worry. In India we saw it happen soon after the nuclear tests in 1998 and during the Kargil War against Pakistan in 1999. In the US we saw it during the Gulf War and we see it now, during the "War On Terror." That blizzard of Made-in-China American flags.[3]

Those who have criticized the actions of the US government (myself included) have been called "anti-American."

Anti-Americanism is in the process of being consecrated as an ideology. The term "anti-American" is usually used by the American establishment to discredit and, not falsely – but, shall we say, inaccurately – define its critics. Once someone is branded anti-American, the chances are that he or she will be judged before they're heard and the argument will be lost in the welter of bruised national pride.

What does the term "anti-American" *mean*? Does it mean you're anti-jazz? Or that you're opposed to free speech? That you don't delight in Toni Morrison or John Updike? That you have a quarrel with giant Sequoias? Does it mean you don't admire the hundreds of thousands of American citizens who marched against nuclear weapons, or the thousands of war resisters who forced their government to withdraw from Vietnam? Does it mean that you hate all Americans?

This sly conflation of America's culture, music, literature, the breathtaking physical beauty of the land, the ordinary pleasures of ordinary people with criticism of the US government's foreign policy (about which, thanks to America's "free press," sadly most Americans know very little) is a deliberate and extremely effective strategy. It's like a retreating army taking cover in a heavily populated city, hoping that the prospect of hitting civilian targets will deter enemy fire.

There are many Americans who are mortified to be associated with their government's policies. The most scholarly, scathing, incisive, hilarious critiques of the hypocrisy and the contradictions in US government policy come from American citizens. When the rest of the world wants to know what the US government is up to, we turn to Noam Chomsky, Howard Zinn, Ed Herman, Amy Goodman, Michael Albert, Chalmers Johnson, William Blum and Anthony Arnove to tell us what's really going on.

Similarly, in India, not hundreds, but millions of us would be ashamed and offended if we were in any way implicated with the present Indian government's fascist policies which, apart from the perpetration of State terrorism in the valley of Kashmir (in the name of fighting terrorism), have also turned a blind eye to the recent state-supervised pogrom against Muslims in Gujarat.[4] It would be absurd to think that those who criticize the Indian government are "anti-Indian" – although the government itself never hesitates to take that line. It is dangerous to cede to the Indian government or the American government or *anyone* for that matter, the right to define what "India" or "America" is, or ought to be.

To call someone "anti-American," indeed, to *be* anti-American, (or for that matter anti-Indian, or anti-Timbuktuan) is not just racist, it's a failure of the imagination. An inability to see the world in terms other than those that the establishment has set out for you: If you're not a Bushie, you're a Taliban. If you don't love us, you hate us. If you're not Good, you're Evil. If you're not with us, you're with the terrorists.

At first, like many others, I too made the mistake of scoffing at this post-September 11th rhetoric, dismissing it as foolish and arrogant. And then I realized that it wasn't foolish at all, but actually a canny recruitment drive for a misconceived, dangerous war. After the invasion of Afghanistan in October 2001, I was constantly taken aback at how many people believed – and still believe – that opposing the war amounted to supporting terrorism, or voting for the Taliban. When the initial aim of the war – capturing Osama bin Laden (dead or alive) – ran into bad weather, the goal posts were moved.[5] It was made out that the whole point of the war was to topple the Taliban regime and liberate Afghan women from their burqas, and we were asked to believe that the US marines are actually on a feminist mission. (If so, perhaps at some stage they'll train their sights on America's military ally Saudi Arabia?) Think of it this way: In India there are some pretty reprehensible social practices, against "untouchables," against Christians and Muslims, against women. Pakistan and Bangladesh have even worse ways of dealing with minority communities and women. Should they be bombed? Should Delhi, Islamabad, and Dhaka be destroyed? Is it possible to bomb bigotry out of India? Can we bomb our way to a feminist paradise? Is that how women won the vote in the United States? Or how slavery was abolished? Can we win redress for the genocide of the millions of Native Americans upon whose corpses the United States was founded by bombing Santa Fe?

None of us need anniversaries to remind us of what we cannot forget. So it is no more than co-incidence that I happen to be here, on American soil, in September – this month of dreadful anniversaries. Uppermost on everybody's mind of course, particularly here in America, is the horror of what has come to be known as 9/11. Three thousand civilians lost their lives in that lethal terrorist strike.[6] The grief is still deep. The rage still sharp. The tears have not dried. And a strange, deadly war is raging around the world. Yet, each person who has lost a loved one surely knows secretly, deeply, that no war, no act of revenge, no daisy-cutters dropped on someone else's loved ones or someone else's children will blunt the edges of their pain or bring their own loved ones back. War cannot avenge those who have died. War is only a brutal desecration of their memory.

What we are seeing now is a vulgar display of the *business* of grief, the commerce of grief, the pillaging of even the most private human feelings for political purposes. It is a terrible, violent thing for a State to do to its people.

What I would really love to talk to you about is Loss. Loss and losing. Grief, failure, brokenness, numbness, uncertainty, fear, the death of feeling, the death of dreaming. The absolute, relentless, endless, habitual unfairness of the world. What does loss mean to individuals? What does it mean to whole cultures, whole peoples who have learned to live with it as a constant companion?

Since it is September 11 that we're talking about, perhaps it's in the fitness of things that we remember what that date means, not only to those who lost their loved ones in America that day, but to those in other parts of the world to whom the date has long held significance. This historical dredging is not offered as an accusation or a provocation. But just to share the grief of history. To thin the mist a little. To say to the citizens of America, in the gentlest, most human way: Welcome to the World.

Thirty-four years ago, in Chile, on September 11 1973, General Pinochet overthrew the democratically elected government of Salvador Allende in a CIA-backed coup. "I don't see why we need to stand by and watch a country go Communist due to the irresponsibility of its own people," said Henry Kissinger, Nobel Peace Laureate, then President Nixon's national security adviser.[7]

After the coup President Allende was found dead inside the presidential palace. Whether he was killed or whether he killed himself, we'll never know. In the regime of terror that ensued, thousands of people were killed. Many more simply "disappeared." Firing squads conducted public executions. Concentration camps and torture chambers were opened across the country. The dead were buried in mine shafts and unmarked graves. For more than sixteen years the people of Chile lived in dread of the midnight knock, of routine "disappearances," of sudden arrest and torture.[8]

In 2000, following the 1998 arrest of General Pinochet in Britain, thousands of secret documents were declassified by the US government.[9] They contain unequivocal evidence of the CIA's involvement in the coup, as well as the fact that the US government had detailed information about the situation in Chile during General Pinochet's reign. Yet Kissinger assured the general of his support. "In the United States, as you know, we are sympathetic with what you are trying to do," he said, "We wish your government well."[10]

Those of us who have only ever known life in a democracy, however flawed, would find it hard to imagine what living in a dictatorship and enduring the absolute loss of freedom really means. It isn't just those who Pinochet murdered, but the lives he stole from the living that must be accounted for too.

Sadly, Chile was not the only country in South America to be singled out for the US government's attentions. Guatemala, Costa Rica, Ecuador, Brazil, Peru, the Dominican Republic, Bolivia, Nicaragua, Honduras, Panama, El Salvador, Peru, Mexico and Colombia – they've all been the playground for covert – and overt – operations by the CIA.[11] Hundreds of thousands of Latin Americans have been killed, tortured, or have simply disappeared under the despotic regimes and tin-pot dictators, drug runners, and arms dealers that were propped up in their countries. (Many of them learned their craft in the infamous US government-funded School of the Americas in Fort Benning, Georgia, which has produced 60,000 graduates.)[12] If this were not humiliation enough, the people of South America have had to bear the cross of being branded as a people who are incapable of democracy – as if coups and massacres are somehow encrypted in their genes.

This list does not, of course, include countries in Africa or Asia that suffered US military interventions – Somalia, Vietnam, Korea, Indonesia, Laos, and Cambodia.[13] For how many Septembers for decades together have millions of Asian people been bombed, burned, and slaughtered? How many Septembers have gone by since August 1945, when hundreds of thousands of ordinary Japanese people were obliterated by the nuclear strikes in Hiroshima and Nagasaki? For how many Septembers have the thousands who had the misfortune of surviving those strikes endured the living hell that was visited on them, their unborn children, their children's children, on the earth, the sky, the wind, the water, and all the creatures that swim and walk and crawl and fly? In Albuquerque, New Mexico, is the National Atomic Museum where Fat Man and Little Boy (the affectionate nicknames for the bombs that were dropped on Hiroshima and Nagasaki) were available as souvenir earrings. Funky young people wore them. A massacre dangling in each ear. But I am straying from my theme. It's September that we're talking about, not August.

September 11 has a tragic resonance in the Middle East too. On September 11 1922, ignoring Arab outrage, the British government proclaimed a mandate in Palestine, a follow-up to the 1917 Balfour Declaration, which Imperial Britain issued with its army massed outside the gates of the city of Gaza.[14] The Balfour Declaration promised European Zionists "a national home for Jewish people."[15] (At the time, the Empire on which the Sun Never Set was free to snatch and bequeath national homes like the school bully distributes marbles.) Two years after the declaration, Lord Arthur James Balfour, the British foreign secretary said, "[I]n Palestine we do not propose even to go through the form of consulting the wishes of the present inhabitants of the country . . . Zionism, be it right or wrong, good or bad, is rooted in age-long tradition, in present needs, in future hopes, of far profounder import than the desires and prejudices of the 700,000 Arabs who now inhabit that ancient land."[16]

How carelessly imperial power decreed whose needs were profound and whose were not. How carelessly it vivisected ancient civilizations. Palestine and Kashmir are Imperial Britain's festering, blood-drenched gifts to the modern world. Both are fault-lines in the raging international conflicts of today.

In 1937 Winston Churchill said of the Palestinians:

> I do not agree that the dog in a manger has the final right to the manger, even though he may have lain there for a very long time. I do not admit that right. I do not admit, for instance, that a great wrong has been done to the Red Indians of America, or the black people of Australia. I do not admit that a wrong has been done to these people by the fact that a stronger race, a higher grade race, a more worldly-wise race, to put it that way, has come in and taken their place.[17]

That set the trend for the Israeli State's attitude towards Palestinians. In 1969, Israeli Prime Minister Golda Meir said, "Palestinians do not exist." Her successor, Prime Minister Levi Eshkol, said, "Where are Palestinians? When I came here [to Palestine] there were 250,000 non-Jews, mainly Arabs and Bedouins. It was desert, more than underdeveloped. Nothing." Prime Minister Menachem Begin called Palestinians "two-legged beasts." Prime Minister Yitzhak Shamir called them " 'grasshoppers' who could be crushed."[18] This is the language of Heads of State, not the words of ordinary people

In 1947 the UN formally partitioned Palestine and allotted 55 percent of Palestine's land to the Zionists. Within a year they had captured more than 76 percent.[19] On May 14 1948 the State of Israel was declared. Minutes after the declaration, the United States and Russia recognized Israel. The West Bank was annexed by Jordan. The Gaza strip came under the military control of Egypt.[20] Formally, Palestine ceased to exist except in the minds and hearts of the hundreds of thousands of Palestinian people who became refugees.

In the summer of 1967, Israel occupied the West Bank and the Gaza Strip. Settlers were offered state subsidies and development aid to move into the occupied territories. And today, almost every day, more Palestinian families are forced off their lands and driven into refugee camps. Palestinians who continue to live in Israel do not have the same rights as Israelis and live as second-class citizens in their former homeland.[21]

Over the decades there have been uprisings, wars, *intifadas*. Thousands have lost their lives.[22] Accords and treaties have been signed. Cease-fires declared and violated. But the bloodshed doesn't end. Palestine still remains illegally occupied. Its people live in inhuman conditions, in virtual Bantustans, where they are subjected to collective punishments, twenty-four hour curfews; where they are humiliated and brutalized on a daily basis. They never know when their homes will be demolished, when their children will be shot, when their precious trees will be cut, when their roads will be closed, when they will be allowed to walk down to the market to buy food and medicine. And when they will not. They live with no semblance of dignity. With not much hope in sight. They have no control over their lands, their security, their movement, their communication, their water supply. So when accords are signed and words like "autonomy" and even "statehood" are bandied about, it's always worth asking: What sort of autonomy? What sort of state? What sort of rights will its citizens have?

Young Palestinians who cannot contain their anger turn themselves into human bombs and haunt Israel's streets and public places, blowing themselves up, killing ordinary people, injecting terror into daily life, and eventually hardening both societies' suspicion and mutual hatred of each other. Each bombing invites merciless reprisals and even more hardship on Palestinian people. But then suicide bombing is an act of individual despair, not a revolutionary tactic. Although Palestinian attacks strike terror into Israeli civilians, they provide the perfect cover for the Israeli government's daily incursions into Palestinian territory, the perfect excuse for old-fashioned, nineteenth-century colonialism, dressed up as a new-fashioned, twenty-first century "war."

Israel's staunchest political and military ally is and always has been the US government. The US government has blocked, along with Israel, almost every UN resolution that sought a peaceful, equitable solution to the conflict.[23] It has supported almost every war that Israel has fought. When Israel attacks Palestine, it is American missiles that smash through Palestinian homes. And every year Israel receives several billion dollars from the United States.[24]

What lessons should we draw from this tragic conflict? Is it really impossible for Jewish people who suffered so cruelly themselves – more cruelly perhaps than any other people in history – to understand the vulnerability and the yearning of those whom they have displaced? Does extreme suffering always kindle cruelty? What hope does this leave the human race with? What will happen to the Palestinian people in the event of a victory? When a nation without a state eventually proclaims a state, what kind of state will it be? What horrors will be perpetrated under its flag? Is it a separate state that we should be fighting for, or the rights to a life of liberty and dignity for everyone, regardless of their ethnicity or religion?

Palestine was once a secular bulwark in the Middle East. But now the weak, undemocratic, by all accounts corrupt but avowedly non-sectarian PLO, is losing ground to Hamas, which espouses an overtly sectarian ideology and fights in the name of Islam. To quote from their manifesto: We will be its soldiers and the firewood of its fire, which will burn the enemies.[25]

The world is called upon to condemn suicide bombers. But can we ignore the long road they have journeyed on before they arrived at this destination? September 11 1922 to September 11 2007 – eighty-five years is a long, long time to have been waging war. Is there some advice the world can give the people of Palestine? Some scrap of hope we can hold out? Should they just settle for the crumbs that are thrown their way and behave like the grasshoppers or two-legged beasts they've been described as? Should they just take Golda Meir's suggestion and make a real effort to not exist?

In another part of the Middle East, September 11 strikes a more recent chord. It was on September 11 1990 that George Bush Sr, then President of the United States, made a speech to a joint session of Congress announcing his Government's decision to go to war against Iraq for the first time.[26]

The US government says that Saddam Hussein is a war criminal, a cruel military despot who has committed genocide against his own people. That's a fairly accurate description of the man. In 1988 he razed hundreds of villages in northern Iraq and used chemical weapons and machine-guns to kill thousands of Kurdish people. Today we know that in that same year the US government provided him with $500 million in subsidies to buy American agricultural products. The next year, after he had successfully completed his genocidal campaign, the US government doubled its subsidy to $1 billion.[27] It also provided him with high-quality germ seed for anthrax, as well as helicopters and dual-use material that could be used to manufacture chemical and biological weapons.[28]

So it turns out that while Saddam Hussein was carrying out his worst atrocities, the US and the UK governments were his close allies. Even today, the government of Turkey, which has one of the most appalling human rights records in the world, is one of the US government's closest allies. The fact that the Turkish government has oppressed and murdered Kurdish people for years has not prevented the US government from plying Turkey with weapons and Development Aid.[29] Clearly it was not concern for the Kurdish people that provoked President Bush's speech to Congress.

What changed? In August 1990, Saddam Hussein invaded Kuwait. His sin was not so much that he had committed an act of war, but that he acted independently, without orders from his masters. This display of independence was enough to upset the power equation in the Gulf. So it was decided that Saddam Hussein must be exterminated, like a pet that has outlived its owner's affection.

Wars are never fought for altruistic reasons. They're usually fought for hegemony, for business. And then of course there's the business of war. Protecting its control of the world's oil is fundamental to US foreign policy. The US government's recent military interventions in the Balkans and Central Asia, and its continuing destruction of Iraq, have to do with oil. Hamid Karzai, the puppet president of Afghanistan installed by the US, is said to be a former employee of Unocal, the American-based oil company.[30] The US government's paranoid patrolling of the Middle

East is because the region has two-thirds of the world's oil reserves.[31] Oil keeps America's engines purring sweetly. Oil keeps the Free Market rolling. Whoever controls the world's oil controls the world's market. And how do you control the oil?

Nobody put it more elegantly than *New York Times* columnist Thomas Friedman. In an article titled "Craziness Pays" he says, "The US has to make clear to Iraq and US allies that . . . America will use force, without negotiation, hesitation, or UN approval."[32] His advice was well taken. In the wars against Iraq and Afghanistan, as well as in the almost daily humiliation the US government heaps upon the UN. In his book on globalization, *The Lexus and the Olive Tree,* Friedman says, "The hidden hand of the market will never work without a hidden fist. McDonald's cannot flourish without McDonnell Douglas . . . And the hidden fist that keeps the world safe for Silicon Valley's technologies to flourish is called the US Army, Air Force, Navy, and Marine Corps."[33] Perhaps this was written in a moment of vulnerability, but it's certainly the most succinct, accurate description of the project of Corporate Globalization that I have read.

After September 11 2001, and in the War On Terror, the hidden hand and fist have had their cover blown and we have a clear view of America's other weapon – the Free Market – bearing down on the Developing World with a clenched unsmiling smile. The Task That Does Not End is America's perfect war, the perfect vehicle for the endless expansion of American Imperialism. In Urdu, the word for "profit" is *fayda. Al Qaeda* means "the Word, the Word of God, the Law." So, in India some of us call the War On Terror, *Al Qaeda v. Al Fayda* – The Word *v.* The Profit (no pun intended).

For the moment it looks as though *Al Fayda* will carry the day. But then again, you never know . . .

In the last fifteen years of unbridled Corporate Globalization, the world's total income has increased by an average of 2.5 percent a year. And yet the number of the poor in the world has increased by 100 million. Of the top hundred biggest economies, fifty-one are corporations, not countries. The top 1 percent of the world has the same combined income as the bottom 57 percent and the disparity is growing.[34] Now, under the expansive canopy of the War On Terror, this process is being hustled along. The men in suits are in an unseemly hurry. While bombs rain down on us, and cruise missiles skid across the skies, while nuclear weapons are stockpiled to make the world a safer place, contracts are being signed, patents are being registered, oil pipelines are being laid, natural resources are being plundered, water is being privatized and democracies are being undermined.

In a country like India, the "structural adjustment" end of the Corporate Globalization project is ripping through people's lives. "Development" projects, massive privatization, and labor "reforms" are pushing people off their lands and out of their jobs, resulting in a kind of barbaric dispossession that has few parallels in history. Across the world, as the Free Market brazenly protects Western markets and forces developing countries to lift their trade barriers, the poor are getting poorer and the rich richer. Civil unrest has begun to erupt in the global village. In countries like Argentina, Brazil, Mexico, Bolivia, and India the resistance movements against Corporate Globalization are growing. To contain them, governments are tightening their control. Protestors are being labeled "terrorists" and then being dealt with as such. But civil unrest does not only mean marches and demonstrations and protests against globalization. Unfortunately, it also means a desperate downward spiral into crime and chaos and all kinds of despair and disillusionment which, as we know from history (and from what we see unspooling before our eyes), gradually becomes a fertile breeding ground for terrible things – cultural nationalism, religious bigotry, fascism and, of course, terrorism.

All these march arm in arm with Corporate Globalization.

There is a notion gaining credence that the Free Market breaks down national barriers, and that Corporate Globalization's ultimate destination is a hippie paradise where the heart is the only passport and we all live together happily inside a John Lennon song (*Imagine there's no country . . .*) This is a canard.

What the Free Market undermines is not national sovereignty, but *democracy*. As the disparity between the rich and poor grows, the hidden fist has its work cut out for it. Multinational corporations on the prowl for "sweetheart deals" that yield enormous profits cannot push through those deals and administer those projects in developing countries without the active connivance of State machinery – the police, the courts, sometimes even the army. Today Corporate Globalization needs an international confederation of loyal, corrupt, authoritarian governments in poorer countries to push through unpopular reforms and quell the mutinies. It needs a press that pretends to be free. It needs courts that pretend to dispense justice. It needs nuclear bombs, standing armies, sterner immigration laws, and watchful coastal patrols to make sure that it is only money, goods, patents and services that are globalized – not the free movement of people, not a respect for human rights, not international treaties on racial discrimination or chemical and nuclear weapons, or greenhouse gas emissions, climate change, or, god forbid, justice.[35] It's as though even a *gesture* towards

international accountability would wreck the whole en-
terprise.

Since the War On Terror was officially flagged off in the
ruins of Afghanistan, in country after country freedoms
have been – and continue to be – curtailed in the name of
protecting freedom; civil liberties are being suspended in the
name of protecting democracy.[36] All kinds of dissent are
being defined as "terrorism." All kinds of laws are being
passed to deal with it. Osama bin Laden seems to have
vanished into thin air. Mullah Omar is said to have made
his escape on a motor-bike.[37] (They could have sent Tintin
after him.) The Taliban disappeared for a while, but have
now resurfaced in southern Afghanistan; moreover their
spirit, and their system of summary justice, are surfacing in
the unlikeliest of places. In India, in Pakistan, in Nigeria, in
America, in all the Central Asian Republics run by all
manner of despots, and, of course, in Afghanistan under
the US-backed Northern Alliance.[38]

Meanwhile down at the Mall there's a mid-season sale.
Everything's discounted – oceans, rivers, oil, gene pools, fig
wasps, flowers, childhoods, aluminum factories, phone
companies, wisdom, wilderness, civil rights, ecosystems,
air – all 4,600 million years of evolution. It's packed, sealed,
tagged, valued and available off the rack. (No returns.) As
for justice – I'm told it's on offer too. You can get the best
that money can buy.

The former US Secretary of Defense Donald Rumsfeld
said that his mission in the War On Terror was to persuade
the world that Americans must be allowed to continue their
way of life.[39] When the maddened King stamps his foot,
slaves tremble in their quarters. So, standing here today, it's
hard for me to say this, but "The American Way of Life" is
simply not sustainable. Because it doesn't acknowledge that
there is a world beyond America.

Fortunately power has a shelf life. When the time comes, maybe this mighty empire will, like others before it, overreach itself and implode from within. It looks as though structural cracks have already appeared. As the War On Terror casts its net wider and wider, America's corporate heart is hemorrhaging. For all the endless empty chatter about democracy, today the world is run by three of the most secretive institutions in the world: the International Monetary Fund, the World Bank, and the World Trade Organization, all three of which, in turn, are dominated by the US. Their decisions are made in secret. The people who head them are appointed behind closed doors. Nobody really knows anything about them, their politics, their beliefs, their intentions. Nobody elected them. Nobody said they could make decisions on our behalf. A world run by a handful of greedy bankers and CEOs who nobody elected can't possibly last.

Soviet-style communism failed, not because it was intrinsically evil but because it was flawed. It allowed too few people to usurp too much power. Twenty-first century market-capitalism, American-style, will fail for the same reasons. Both are edifices constructed by human intelligence, undone by human nature.

The time has come, the Walrus said. Perhaps things will get worse and then better. Perhaps there's a small god up in heaven readying herself for us. Another world is not only possible, she's on her way. Maybe many of us won't be here to greet her, but on a quiet day, if I listen very carefully, I can hear her breathing.

NOTES

1. J. Berger, *Ways of Seeing* (New York: Penguin, 1990).
2. D. Johnston, "U.S. Hits Back Inspirations," *The Advertiser,* September 22 2001, p. 7.
3. J. Pomfret, "Chinese Working Overtime to Sew U.S. Flags," *Washington Post,* September 20 2001, p. A14.
4. A. Roy, "Democracy: Who Is She When She's at Home," in *The Algebra of Infinite Justice* (New Delhi: Penguin, 2002).
5. D. E. Sanger, "Bin Laden Is Wanted in Attacks, 'Dead or Alive,' President Says," *New York Times,* September 18 2001, p. A1; J. F. Burns, "10-Month Afghan Mystery: Is bin Laden Dead or Alive?" *New York Times,* September 30 2002, p. A1.
6. See the Associated Press database of those confirmed dead, reported dead or reported missing in the September 11 terrorist attacks. Available at: http://attacksvictims.ap.org/totals.asp
7. S. M. Hersh, *The Price of Power: Kissinger in the Nixon White House* (New York: Summit, 1983), p. 265.
8. P. Aguilera, A. Dorfman, and R. Fredes (eds), *Chile: The Other September 11* (New York: Ocean, 2002); "The Case of Augusto Pinochet," *Amnesty International.* Available at: http://www.amnestyusa.org/countries/chile/pinochet_case.html
9. C. Krauss, "Britain Arrests Pinochet to Face Charges by Spain," *New York Times,* October 18 1998, p. 1:1; "Chile: 16,000 Secret U.S. Documents Declassified," Press Release, *National Security Archive*, November 13 2000 Available at: http://www.gwu.edu/~nsarchiv/news/20001113/; and selected documents on the National Security Archive. Available at: http://www.gwu.edu/~nsarchiv/news/20001113/#docs
10. Kissinger told this to Pinochet at a meeting of the Organization of American States in Santiago, Chile, on June 8 1976. See L. Kosimar, "Kissinger Covered Up Chile Torture," *Observer,* February 28 1999, p. 3.
11. Among other histories, see E. Galeano, *Open Veins of Latin America: Five Centuries of the Pillage of a Continent,* 2nd edn, trans. Cedric Belfrage (New York: Monthly Review,

1998); N. Chomsky, *Turning the Tide: U.S. Intervention in Central America and the Struggle for Peace*, 2nd edn (Boston: South End, 1985); N. Chomsky, *The Culture of Terrorism* (Boston: South End, 1983); and G. Kolko, *Confronting the Third World: United States Foreign Policy, 1945–1980* (New York: Pantheon, 1988).

12. In a public relations move, the SOA renamed itself the Western Hemisphere Institute for Security Cooperation (WHISC) on January 17 2001. See J. Nelson-Pallmeyer, *School of Assassins: Guns, Greed, and Globalization*, 2nd ed. (New York: Orbis, 2001); M. Gormley, "Army School Faces Critics Who Call It Training Ground for Assassins," *Associated Press*, May 2 1998; and School of the Americas Watch (http://www.soaw.org).

13. On these interventions, see, among other sources, N. Chomsky, *American Power and the New Mandarins*, 2nd ed. (New York: New Press, 2002); N. Chomsky, *At War With Asia* (New York: Vintage, 1970); and H. Zinn, *Vietnam: The Logic Of Withdrawal*, 2nd ed. (Cambridge, MA: South End, 2002).

14. S. K. Farsoun and C. E. Zacharia, *Palestine and the Palestinians* (Boulder, CO: Westview, 1997), p. 10.

15. The Balfour Declaration can be found in ibid., Appendix 2, p. 320.

16. N. Chomsky, *Fateful Triangle: The United States, Israel, and the Palestinians*, 2nd ed. (Cambridge, MA: South End, 2000), p. 90.

17. Quoted in Editorial, "Scurrying Towards Bethlehem," *New Left Review* 10, 2nd series (July/August 2001), p. 9, n. 5.

18. Farsoun and Zacharia, *op.cit.*, pp. 10 and 243.

19. Ibid., pp. 111 and 123.

20. Ibid., p. 116.

21. See Chomsky, *Fateful Triangle*, pp. 103–107, 118–32, and 156–60.

22. From 1987 to 2002 alone, more than 2,000 Palestinians have been killed. See B'Tselem (The Israeli Information Center for Human Rights in the Occupied Territories), "Palestinians Killed in the Occupied Territories," table. Available at: http://www.btselem.org/English/Statistics/Total_Casualties.asp

23. See N. H. Aruri, *Dishonest Broker: The U.S. Role in Israel and Palestine* (Cambridge, MA: South End, forthcoming); N. Chomsky, *World Orders Old and New*, 2nd ed. (New York: Columbia University Press, 1996).

24. In addition to more than $3 billion annually in official Foreign Military Financing (FMF), the US government supplies Israel with economic assistance, loans, technology transfers, and arms sales. See N. Anderson, "House Panel Increases Aid for Israel, Palestinians," *Los Angeles Times*, May 10 2002, p. A1; N. H. Aruri, *Dishonest Broker*, Appendix 1 and Appendix 2; and A. Arnove and A. Shawki, "Foreword," *The Struggle for Palestine*, ed. L. Selfa (Chicago: Haymarket, 2002), p. xxv.

25. Article 27 of the Charter of the Islamic Resistance Movement (Hamas), quoted in Farsoun and Zacharia, *op.cit.*, Appendix 13, p. 339.

26. G. W. Bush, "Text of Bush's Speech: 'It Is Iraq Against the World,'" *Los Angeles Times*, September 12 1990, p. A7.

27. G. Frankel, "Iraq Long Avoided Censure on Rights," *Washington Post*, September 22 1990, p. A1.

28. C. Dickey and E. Thomas, "How Saddam Happened," *Newsweek*, September 23 2002, pp. 35–37.

29. A. Arnove, "Introduction," *Iraq Under Siege: The Deadly Impact of Sanctions and War*, 2nd edn, ed. A. Arnove (Cambridge, MA: South End; London: Pluto, 2002), p. 20.

30. See P. Watson, "Afghanistan Aims to Revive Pipeline Plans," *Los Angeles Times*, May 30 2002, p. A1; I. R. Prusher, S. Baldauf, and E. Girardet, "Afghan Power Brokers," *Christian Science Monitor*, June 10 2002, p. 1.

31. See L. Fingeret et al., "Markets Worry That Conflict Could Spread in Area That Holds Two-Thirds of World Reserves," *Financial Times* (London), April 2 2002, p. 1.

32. T. L. Friedman, "Craziness Pays," *New York Times*, February 24 1998, p. A21.

33. T. L. Friedman, *The Lexus and the Olive Tree: Understanding Globalization* (New York: Farrar, Strauss, and Giroux, 1999), p. 373.

34. Statistics from J. E. Stiglitz, *Globalization and Its Discontents* (New York and London: W.W. Norton, 2002), p. 5; N. Chomsky, *Rogue States: The Rule of Law in World Affairs*

(Cambridge, MA: South End Press, 2000), p. 214; and N. Hertz, "Why Consumer Power Is Not Enough," *New Statesman,* April 30 2001.

35. Among the many treaties and international agreements the United States has not signed, ignores, violates, or has broken are: UN International Covenant on Economic, Social and Cultural Rights (1966); the UN Convention on the Rights of the Child (CRC); the UN Convention on the Elimination of All Forms of Discrimination Against Women (CEDAW); agreements setting the jurisdiction for the International Criminal Court (ICC); the 1972 Anti-Ballistic Missile Treaty with Russia; the Comprehensive Test Ban Treaty (CTBT); and the Kyoto Protocol regulating greenhouse gas emissions.

36. D. Cole and J. X. Dempsey, *Terrorism and the Constitution: Sacrificing Civil Liberties in the Name of National Security* (New York: New Press, 2002).

37. L. Harding, "Elusive Mullah Omar 'Back in Afghanistan'," *Guardian*, August 30 2002, p. 12.

38. See Human Rights Watch, "Opportunism in the Face of Tragedy: Repression in the Name of Anti-Terrorism." Available at: http://www.hrw.org/campaigns/september11/opportunismwatch.htm

39. A. Roy, "The Algebra of Infinite Justice," in *The Algebra of Infinite Justice* (New Delhi: Penguin, 2002).

JOHN BERGER

Human Shield

How this letter came into my hands must remain a secret.

Mi Guapo,

I'm not going to send you this letter, yet I want to tell you what we did the other day. Perhaps you won't read it until we are both dead, no, the dead don't read. The dead are what remains from what has been written. Much of what is written is reduced to ashes. The dead are all there in the words that stay.

Tonight you are listening in your cell to my words as I write. I'm sitting up in bed. The pad is on my knees.

If I close my eyes I see your ears, the left one sticking out more than the right. My elder sister used to claim that human ears are like dictionaries and that, if you know how, you can look up words in them.

Limpid, for instance, Limpid.

My mobile rang and there was Yasmina's clipped voice – finches chirp quickly like this when their tree is at risk – telling me that an Apache had been circling above the old tobacco factory in the Abor district, where seven of ours were hiding, and that the neighboring women – and other women too – were preparing to form a human shield around the factory and on its roof, to prevent them shelling it. I told her I would come.

I put down the telephone and stood still, yet it was as if I was running. Cool air was striking my forehead. Something of mine – but not my body, maybe my name, A'ida – was running, swerving, soaring, plummeting and becoming impossible to sight or get aim on. Perhaps a released bird has this sensation. A kind of limpidity.

By the time I got there, twenty women, waving white headscarves, were installed on the flat roof. The factory has three floors – like your prison. At ground level, lines of women with their backs to the wall surrounded the entire building. No tanks, jeeps, or Humvees yet to be seen. So I walked from the road across the wasteland to join them.

Some of the women I recognized, others I didn't. We touched and looked at one another silently, to confirm what we shared, what we had in common. Our one chance was to become a single body for as long as we stood there and refused to budge.

We heard the Apache returning. It was flying slowly and low to frighten and observe us, its four-bladed rotor blackmailing the air below to hold it up. We heard the familiar Apache growl, the growl of them deciding and us rushing for shelter to hide – but not today. An Apache weighs nine tons. We could see the two Hellfire missiles tucked under its armpits. We could see the pilot and his gunner. We could see the mini-guns pointing at us.

Before the ruined mountain, before the abandoned factory, which was used as a makeshift hospital during the dysentery epidemic four years ago, some of us were likely to die. Each of us, I think, was frightened but not for herself.

Other women were hurrying down the zigzag path from the heights of Mount Abor. It's very steep there – you remember? – and they couldn't see the helicopter. They were holding on to each other and shrieking with laughter. It was strange to hear their laughter and the growling drone

of the Apache together. I looked along the line of my
companions, particularly at their foreheads, and I was
convinced that some of them had felt something like I
had. Their foreheads were limpid. When the stragglers from
Mount Abor reached us, they adjusted their clothes and we
warmly and solemnly embraced them.

The more we are, the larger the target we make, and the
larger the target, the stronger we are. A weird, limpid logic!
Each of us was frightened but not for herself.

The Apache was hovering above the factory roof, three
floors higher in the sky, stationary but never still. We held
one another's hands and from time to time repeated each
other's names. I was holding the hands of Koto and Miriam.
Koto was nineteen and had very white teeth. Miriam was a
widow in her fifties whose husband had been killed twenty
years ago. Although I'm not going to send you this letter I
change their names.

At that moment we heard the tanks approaching down
the street. Four of them. PD9s. Koto was stroking my wrist
with one of her fingers. We heard a Tannoy voice announcing a curfew and ordering everyone to disperse and get
indoors. The street on the other side of the wasteland was
crowded, and I spotted several cameramen there. A few
decigrams in our favor.

The immense PD9s were now coming fast towards us,
turrets turning to select their exact direction. The fear
provoked by sounds is the hardest to control. The clatter
of their tracks grappling and flattening whatever they drove
over, the roar of their 1500 horsepower engines twisted into
a suction noise, and the Modular Crowd Control Speaker
ordering us to disperse – all three becoming louder and
louder, until they stopped in a line facing us, twelve metres
away, and the muzzles of their 105mm cannons even closer.
We didn't huddle, we stood apart, only our hands touching.

A commander emerging from the hatch of the first tank informed us, speaking our language badly, that we would now be forced to disperse.

Do you know how much an Apache costs? I asked Koto out of the corner of my mouth. She shook her head. Fifty million dollars, I said between my teeth. Miriam kissed my cheek. I was expecting the special rear doors of one of the PD9s to be pushed up and six soldiers to emerge, land on their feet and run us down. It would have taken no more than a minute. And it didn't happen. Instead the tanks turned and, following each other with a distance of 20 meters between each, they began slowly to circle our circle.

I didn't think it then, mi Guapo, but now writing to you in the middle of the night, I think of Herodotus. Herodotus from Halicarnasse, who was the first to write down stories about tyrants being made deaf to every god by the din of their own machines.

We could never have resisted the soldiers, they would have carted us off. The tanks, as they circled us, deliberately drew nearer – they were tightening the noose.

You know how a cat measures her jump, the distance of it, landing on her four feet close together, on the very spot she calculated? This is what each of us had to do, measuring, not the distance of a leap, but its opposite – the precise amount of willpower needed to take the terrifying decision to stay put, to do nothing, despite fear. Nothing. If you underestimated the willpower needed, you'd break line and run before you realized what you were doing. The fear was constant but it fluctuated. If you overestimated, you'd be exhausted and useless before the end and the others would have to prop you up. Our holding hands helped because the calculating energy passed from hand to hand.

When the tanks had circled the factory once, they were no more than an arms length away from us. Through the netted vents of their hulls, helmets, eyes, gloved hands were sometimes visible. The PD9s have a crew of four, apart from the infantry soldiers they can transport in their rear cabin. The commanders were examining us, the others were gazing at their battlefield-screen and weapon-controls.

More fearful than any weapon was the armored plating. It covered turret and hull and four aprons of it hung over the caterpillar tracks and the six wheels, at the height of our hips. When each tank passed, it was this surface, the most impermeable ever created by man, that we couldn't avoid seeing, even if we sang – and we had now started singing – with its rounded blind rivets, its texture of an animal-hide so it never shines, its granite hardness and its shit coloring, the coloring not of a mineral but of decay. It was against this surface that we were waiting to be crushed. And facing this surface we must decide, second by second, not to move, not to budge.

My brother, shouted Koto, my brother says any tank can be destroyed if you find the right place and the right moment!

How were we able – all three hundred of us – to hold out as we did?

The caterpillar treads were now a few centimetres from our sandals. We didn't move. We went on holding hands and singing to each other in our old women's voices. For this is what had happened and this is why we could do what we did. We had not aged, we were simply old, a thousand years old.

A long burst from a machine gun in the street. Positioned as we were, we couldn't see properly what was happening, so we made signs to our old sisters on the roof who could see better than us. The Apache hung menacingly above them. They made signs back and we understood that a patrol had fired on some running figures. Soon we heard the wail of a siren.

The suction of the next tank hemming us in, ruffled and billowed our skirts. Do nothing. We didn't budge our feet. We were terrified. And in our shrill grandmother's voices, we were singing – We're here to stay! Each of us armed with nothing except a derelict uterus.

That's how it was.

Then one tank – we didn't immediately believe our dim eyes – stopped circling and headed off across the wasteland, followed by the next and the next and the next. The old women on the roof cheered, and we, still holding hands but now silent, began to side-step towards the left so that slowly, very slowly as befitted our years, we were circling the factory.

About an hour later, the seven were ready to slip away. We, their grandmothers, dispersed, remembering what it had been like to be young. And within ten minutes I heard the street news, passed from mouth to mouth: Manda, the music teacher, had been shot dead in the street. She had been trying to join us.

The lute is like no other instrument, she once said, as soon as you balance a lute on your lap, it becomes a man! Manda!

For so long as I am alive, I am yours, mi Guapo.

                                                                A'ida

HAIFA ZANGANA

Songs of Iraqi Resistance

"They could kill him, but they couldn't kill his songs."[1]

Midway through the occupation's fifth year, Iraqi popular
opposition to the Anglo- American occupation of the
country, and to its puppet regime under the flimsy guise
of local administration, is increasing in extent and intensity.
The number of Iraqis fighting to expel the occupiers continues to rise; many more provide support and protection to
the armed resistance.

Alongside the armed struggle other kinds of resistance
have developed, especially in the cultural sphere. Various
forms of cultural resistance grow out of the same unbear-
able reality in Iraq, with its almost total lack of services and
security and the daily humiliations that the occupation
brings. This, combined with a natural national impulse
against occupation, is forcing even the most reluctant Iraqis
to join one or other strand of the resistance.

Mass media in the West largely ignores the effectiveness of
the Iraqi resistance against the US's highly advanced tech-
nological war machine,[2] preferring instead to dwell on
intercommunal conflict between sectarian groups. But the
facts, documented and verified on official or reputable web
sites, are unmistakable for anyone who cares to seek them
out.

The occupation's massive propaganda war focusing on sectarian strife complements US and UK counterinsurgency strategies on the ground, which actively promote a sectarian divide-and-rule policy. Most Iraqis in their towns and neighborhoods, however, can clearly distinguish between the clandestine resistance that targets only the occupying forces and their local proxies, and the criminal gangs recruited by the occupiers and their private contractors[3] to terrorize the population and shut down the street life that is the water and air of the urban national resistance. But the occupation's dismantling of civil and state institutions, and the criminality of the new occupation-trained security forces, have given rise to local neighborhood vigilante groups that have proved a mixed blessing. These groups have ended up relying on the support of traditional structures of mosque and tribe, and have at times been manipulated by sectarian parties and militias, with their huge funds and access to the infrastructure of occupation. As a result, some of these vigilante groups have engaged in communal conflict and have been used in criminal counterinsurgency activities, and in the propaganda of occupation.[4] But for most Iraqis, the main aim remains a national and non-sectarian resistance to a foreign occupation.[5] Indeed, the average number of daily attacks on the occupation troops is continually rising, and by June 2007 had reached an average of 185 a day. Without the direct and indirect support of the Iraqi people, this level of resistance would never have been achieved.[6]

Iraqi people are aware that they are paying a very high price for the expansion of the US empire, for reasons other than those declared. They perceive the real motives behind the occupation to be the US's thirst for cheap oil, and the securing of Israel's occupation of Palestine. A recent survey into Iraqi attitudes found "almost no Iraqis who felt the United States had invaded to liberate their country from tyranny and build a democracy." Asked for "the three main reasons for the US invasion of Iraq," fully 76 percent cited "to control Iraqi oil;" followed by "to build military bases" (41 percent), and "to help Israel" (32 percent). Fewer than 2 percent selected "to bring democracy to Iraq" as their first choice.[7]

Iraqis have been on the receiving end of US–UK pledges to establish human rights in the Middle East, pledges that have acquired a grotesque resonance in occupied Iraq, from the torture of detainees in the prisons of Abu Ghraib, Bucca in southern Iraq, Cropper at the US military headquarters at Baghdad airport and the secret prisons of the Ministries of the Interior and of Defence, to the rapid deterioration of health and education services and the lack of basic infrastructure. Freedom of speech, like democracy, was strangled at birth with the systematic assassinations of academics and journalists, and the public murder of clerics.

To justify the arrest, torture and killing of journalists, and to put an end to a free press that threatened to reveal the nature and extent of the crimes committed under occupation, the US administration accused the Iraqi media of being a resource for the "insurgents" and "terrorists" – a resource that needed to be counteracted or contained by all means possible.[8] The occupation's stated objective to aid the establishment of a free press in Iraq has in fact been a mission to establish control over press freedom. The offices of Al Sharqiya Iraqi TV and of Arab TV stations in Baghdad such as Al Arabiya and Al Jazeera, have been raided and shut down. Winning the media war has become an integral part of military strategy.

The surge of US troops, the latest military operation, in which the occupying troops are regularly conducting air strikes in and near population centers,[9] has resulted in

increasing numbers of civilian casualties and further deterioration of the humanitarian situation. Many wounded or
sick people cannot safely access hospitals and clinics.

The number of newly displaced people, both internally and
abroad, stands at 90,000 per month in 2007,[10] and "the
number of people arrested or interned by the multinational
forces has increased by 40% since early 2006. The number of
people held by the Iraqi authorities has also increased significantly."[11] There are over 38,000 detainees in US–UK and
Iraqi detention centers. The ICRC is unable to gain access to
more than 18,000 of these inmates; Iraqi vice-president
Tareq Al Hashemi questioned United States forces over
the fate of 9,000 detainees who, according to US army
statistics, have simply "vanished" from the face of the Earth.
Iraqis think that many might be accounted for among the
bodies of those tortured, blindfolded, and murdered that are
found daily, dumped in various places across the country.

According to a refereed report in the medical journal *The
Lancet*, "Bringing democracy to Iraq" had resulted in the
deaths of 650,000 Iraqis by mid-2006.[12] This is propor-
tionally equivalent to 7 million US citizens or 1.4 million
British citizens. More than half of Iraq's doctors have
already fled the country; Iraqi women are driven to despair
and self-destruction by grief. Their expectations are reduced
to pleas for help to clear the bodies of the dead from the
streets, according to a report by the ICRC.[13]

It is hardly any wonder that most Iraqis approve of
attacks on US-led forces, and that a strong majority wants
US-led military forces to withdraw immediately from the
country, saying that their swift departure would make Iraq
more secure and decrease sectarian violence.[14]

Most surveys and media reports seem to ignore Iraqis'
strong belief that the occupation is also targeting their

national identity, culture, history, language and religion. They ask, "How else can you explain the destruction and looting of the Iraqi museum, which houses the precious artefacts of the world's oldest civilization, as well as of 22 universities and art galleries, the National Library with its unique manuscripts and historical documents, and archaeological sites, while US-led troops either assist looters or watch from a distance?" Is it any wonder that, in the minds of Iraqis, these acts invoke comparison with the barbarity of the Mongols when they sacked Baghdad in 1258?

The killing of academics, scientists, doctors, journalists, singers and artists is seen as an attack on culture and learning. One recent crime is the killing of Khalil al-Zahawi, one of the Muslim world's leading calligraphers, who taught students from all over the Middle East. He was shot dead by gunmen in Baghdad, in late May 2007.

The renowned Iraqi musician Naseer Shamma views the "sovereign new Iraq" thus:

> . . . far from democracy and sovereignty as it has been for decades. Iraq must see the end of foreign intervention, the destruction of its culture, its people and its history . . . The US has simply erased whole segments of what the Iraqis hold dearest; libraries have been burnt, and so has culture – the soul. Americans like to do that: to encroach on a people and destroy its identity.[15]

The silencing of Iraqi intellectuals and cultural figures is what Saadi Youssef, the prominent Iraqi poet, has called "'bullet censorship,' where alongside military and economic colonization there is cultural colonization."[16]

To counteract this colonization and to defend Iraqis' national identity, various modes of cultural resistance have become a powerful weapon in emphasizing that, contrary to what the occupiers would have the world believe, the diversity of Iraq's national identity is rooted in our history; it is a source of our pride in our existence, our history, and our many achievements in the worlds of art, music, science, literature, archaeology and architecture.

One of the most important forms of cultural resistance is song, which is considered particularly influential due to its powerful combination of poetry and music – both highly regarded by Iraqis – its accessibility to the masses, and the impossibility of banning it. Furthermore, the occupiers have found Iraqi singers extremely difficult to recruit – unlike politicians and some journalists.

The occupation and its medieval sectarian proxies fear the influence of *aghani al muqawama*, or songs of resistance. As many as seventy-five well-known singers have been killed since April 2003[17]; music stores selling CDs and DVDs have been ransacked and forced to shut down, while their owners have been arrested or have disappeared, never to be heard of again. Most of these attacks are carried out either directly by the occupation troops or by their mercenaries, and by local militias nurtured by the occupations' puppet government to silence one of the most popular forms of resistance.

In this climate of fear and death, while well-known media personalities, singers, and poets are intimidated and silenced, anonymous resistance songs are widely distributed among the masses. Famous singers continue to contribute from exile, and young people have been inventive in making up new ways to challenge the occupation, so that CDs are replacing the absent voices. Crisis Group Middle East Report noted that:

For increasing numbers of Iraqis, disenchanted with both the US and their own leaders and despairing of their poor living conditions, solace is found in the perceived world of a pious and heroic resistance. CDs that picture the insurrection's exploits can readily be found across the country, new songs glorify combatants, and poems written decades ago during the post-World War I British occupation are getting a new lease of life.

A 1941 poem on Falluja written by Maaruf al-Rusafi has been rediscovered . . . More generally, insurgent videos are widely distributed in mosques and readily available in most Baghdad movie-stores.[18]

In Iraq, poetry has an important political and social role to play. The poet enjoys a special status as the spokesman of his neighborhood, community, tribe or people in general, expressing their hopes, aspirations, and problems. In some cases, the role of the poet is equivalent to that of a journalist or a press officer. In other cases, the poet – be they man or woman – can inspire people to act, to defend their country, or simply to unite and love each other.

Saadi Youssef was asked why he thinks poetry is so central to Middle Eastern culture. He replied that "The oral tradition is very important. Partly this stems from censorship. The first thing to be searched for at Arab airports is not drugs or guns, but books! But poetry you can smuggle across borders. Novels can be censored easily, but poetry stays in the head."[19]

Iraq is also famous for its poetical lyrics and rich musical heritage, which, originating in antiquity, gained sophistication and momentum during the height of the Islamic Empire between the eighth and the thirteenth centuries. The lyrics are either in classical Arabic, the language of the Quran, or local dialect. Among the instruments often used by Iraqi musicians and singers are the *oud* (or lute), the *al-qanoun* (a rectangular stringed instrument), the *tabla* and *daf* (both percussion instruments) and the *nay* (or flute). All these instruments carry the continuity of history.

While they retain strong links with traditional music and classical poetry, modern Iraqi songs of resistance are characterized by their themes, mixed styles, and innovative use of instruments. The songs vary in style and melodic mode from the celebrated Iraqi *maqam*[20] – a complicated melody type sung in both secular and religious contexts, originating in the Abbassid era (750–1258 CE) – to modern pop; and from Sufi-style group chanting to Bedouin-style solo voice, depending on the singer and context of performance, whether it is produced underground inside Iraq (a highly risky activity), or abroad. The dominant and most successful songs are those that adopt the centuries-old Islamic style of chanting by a lead male vocalist singer with a small chorus playing percussion, the *daf* or *riq* (types of tambourine). This kind of chanting is called *al manqaba*, or *al madih al nabawi*, hymns praising the prophet Muhammad that are widespread in all Muslim countries. Chant of this kind transcends sectarian and ethnic divisions within Iraq; it also crosses national boundaries and is deeply rooted in Arab–Islamic culture. The use of this genre by religious and secular singers of the resistance is significant, and has to be seen in the context of the growing need for unity in the face of foreign domination and the planned fragmentation of the people and the country.

Popular singer Sabah Al Janabi was the first to use *al manqaba* tradition to sing about the resistance in Falluja. Others soon followed with themes chosen to inspire people to resist, defend, and celebrate their heritage, identity, religion, homeland; to live with dignity and not to accept the slavery of the invaders. Singers often call for unity and emphasize above all things "Iraqiness," using metaphors and symbols such as the date palm (Iraq's national tree), the

Euphrates and Tigris rivers, and distinguished Iraqi land-marks such as the massive al-Hurriyya (Freedom) monument by the sculptor and painter Jawad Salim, which was erected in Baghdad's Tahrir Square after the 1958 revolution overthrew the British-imposed monarchy. Many singers articulate the suffering, humiliation, and deprivation of life under occupation, depicting the impotence of the occupation and its proxies with black humor; they also express the hopes, aspirations, and spirit of the resistance.

Needless to say, none of these songs are on mainstream radio or TV in Iraq. CDs, DVDs, and videos can be found on the internet and under the counter in the few remaining Iraqi CD shops or are, as we say in Iraq, "saved in our heads." Sometimes, songs are accompanied by videos of images depicting the brutality of the occupation: the destruction of houses, prisoners in Abu Ghraib, dead children, women mourning their loss, and young people – like the Palestinian youths – throwing stones at Humvees and tanks, or celebrating the success of an attack. In most cases, due to the extreme difficulties of clandestine production, only a few basic instruments are used; however, they are skilfully mixed with recorded sounds to produce the noise of air-strikes, bombardment, machine guns, and Apaches hovering in the Iraqi sky.

By late 2003, the occupation had begun to grasp the impact of songs of resistance on the wider Iraqi population. CDs and DVDs were constantly being rushed out and sold in bazaars, at popular stalls in Bab Al Sharqi in the center of Baghdad, and in crowded markets in Al Sadr City. An unsuccessful ban was imposed, as a result of which their popularity increased, particularly among young people. Thereafter music stores were destroyed, singers fled the country or went underground, and the rhetoric of "Islamist" attacks on music stores was hurriedly picked up by the media to cover up the responsibility of the occupation and its sectarian puppets.

In February 2004 a bookseller told *Le Monde*, "A couple of weeks ago, the GIs came. They broke my store window. They turned everything in the store upside down. They arrested my brother. We haven't heard from him since."

They also descended on the Sabah Recordings store and "destroyed everything they could . . . Since then Sabah al-Jenabi has been on the run. Another singer, Abdel Rahman al-Refai, a taxi driver by profession, has disappeared."[21]

Occupation spokesman Dan Senor justified the attacks on newspaper offices, bookshops, and music shops, stating that "any systematic public expression that incites violence against the Coalition is banned." Therefore, singing has been prohibited unless it complies with the occupation's laws.

The ultimate symbol of unity and national identity is the city of Baghdad or, as it had been known historically, Madinat Al Salam (City of Peace), one of the leading cultural centers of the Arab world. Some of the most famous Iraqi sculptors, poets, and writers hail from Baghdad or have graduated from one of its prestigious universities. For us, the city represents the continuity of human achievement and history, and instils in us a feeling of pride and dignity. It is the beating heart of Iraqi culture.

Baghdad is where *maqam* and *pestah* – a kind of light song that concludes a *maqam* – are at their best. Hence the use of this genre to express the anger and disillusionment of Baghdad, often portrayed metaphorically in songs as a young woman or a mother, whose honor Iraqis are failing to defend against the "attacks of the barbarians, the US troops, the moguls of the 21st century."[22]

In one of his songs, the singer and poet Khdhair Hadi describes Baghdad in colloquial Arabic, "Our loved Baghdad is shackled with chains." Sabah Al Janaby sings "We are the wall that protects Baghdad. We never fear for our lives but for Baghdad," while the world's most popular Iraqi singer, Kazem Al-Sahir, instructs his listeners to love the city and dream of her happy face. In a song called "Baghdad," he pleads in classical Arabic to the city not to show her pain while watching her children be killed. In his new song, also entitled "Baghdad," Iraqi pop singer Hussam Al Rassam mixes classical Arabic lyrics with Baghdadi dialect in a heart-rending fusion of Sufi chanting, western choir, and *maqam*, in order to portray the city's plight. Here again, Baghdad is personified as a shy woman appealing to her people to speak up and fight, but Al Rassam extends the metaphor, portraying the city as the child Sakina[23], and as a mother.

Choir [in classical Arabic]: "I hear Baghdad appealing, 'Who is the fighter to avenge my honor?'"

Singer [in Baghdadi dialect]: ". . . indignant, calling her folks to heal her wounds and restore her pride."

Singer: "I am Sakina. Which of you will be my Abbas?"

Continuing with the words "I am mother of churches and mosques/ Whose grounds holy, now despoiled," the singer emphasizes that Baghdad is a city for all Iraqis regardless of their sects or religions. He uses the famous lamentation mode of Shiites at the anniversary of the martyrdom of Imam Hussain – which usually takes place at the holy city of Najaf – to dismiss the possibility of a US victory in Iraq with a simple question: "How could Al-Najaf be Texas?" And the choir states what such a victory would entail for any Iraqi: "They want me to wear different skin."

Al Rassam ends his song with a note of hope, recalling an image from a place of happy memories for Iraqis and visitors alike: "Could only awaken by a tree laughing in Abu Nuwwas."[24]

The resistance of Fallujan people and the almost total destruction of the city, which has prompted comparisons with the Nazis' bombing of the innocents of Guernica, has become one of the symbols of the resistance worldwide. Songs of Falluja, such as "Hay-yalla 'hlil Falluja" ("Salute, O God, the people of Falluja"), is sung in western Iraqi dialect and is dedicated to the courageous resistance of its people, praising their choice to die with dignity rather than live as slaves, and challenging the US troops to approach Falluja again.

From his exile in Egypt, the musician Naseer Shamma remains hopeful; he believes in the Iraqi people, their inherent pride and their capacity to resist injustice, as much as he believes in himself: "No way will they [Iraqis] be silent about the US presence. They will resist until the occupation ends, whatever the price."[25]

As for most Iraqi people, there is only one solution to this disaster and that is for the US and Britain to accept that the Iraqi resistance is fighting to end the occupation. And to acknowledge that it consists largely of ordinary Iraqis, not just Sunnis or Shias, not those "terrorists" – as Tony Blair called them – inspired by neighboring countries such as Iran. It should be recognized that Iraqis are a proud, peace-loving people, and that the main targets of the resistance are not Iraqi civilians – they hate occupation, not each other. And to those who often ask why Iraqi resistance has not got a political program, my answer is: listen to our songs.

NOTES

1. Joan Jara, widow of Chilean singer Victor Jara, in an interview with the BBC, September 5 1998. Victor was arrested on September 11 1973 by the Chilean military, days after the US-backed coup to overthrow the democratic popular unity government of Salvador Allende. The torturer broke his hands so that he could not play his guitar again. His body was dumped on the street.

2. The US President signed a bill on May 26 2007 providing $100 billion to pay for the Iraq war. That is a "supplementary" budget to the already repeatedly overrun costs, estimated to be over $400 billion.

3. Latest estimates on the numbers of mercenaries in Iraq, labeled "private security contractors," is 126,000. *Channel 4 News*, 7 p.m., May 30 2007.

4. Mundher Al Adhami, "Qualitative rise in Iraqi resistance operations and the US counter acts," *Al Quds*, May 19 2007. (Arabic).

5. The Iraqi Surveys, part of the ongoing World Values Surveys, are a collaborative project between the University of Michigan Institute for Social Research and Eastern Michigan University. Available at: http://www.umich.edu/news/index.html?Releases/2006/Jun06/r061406a

6. Brookings Institution Iraq Index. Available at: http://www.brookings.edu/iraqindex

7. The Iraqi Surveys, *op.cit.*

8. Donald Rumsfeld defended "buying news" in Iraq and the use of electronic communications more generally as an important weapon in the war effort. D. H. Rumsfeld, "The Media War on Terror," *Project Syndicate*, April 9, 2006. Available at: http://www.project-syndicate.org/commentary/rumsfeld3

9. CENTAF reported a total of 10,519 "close air support missions" in Iraq in 2006. The Guided Bomb Unit-12, a laser-guided bomb with a 500-pound general purpose warhead – 95 of which were reportedly dropped in 2006 – was the most frequently used bomb in Iraq last year, according to CENTAF.

10. UNHCR estimates there are some 1.9 million Iraqis displaced internally, and up to 2 million in neighboring states, particularly Syria and Jordan. Available at: http://www.unhcr.org/iraq.html

11. "Civilians without Protection: the ever-worsening humanitarian crisis in Iraq," *ICRC Report*, April 11 2007.

12. G. Burnham, R. Lafta, S. Doocy, and L. Roberts, "Mortality after the 2003 invasion of Iraq," *The Lancet*, October 11 2007. Available at: http://www.thelancet.com/webfiles/images/journals/lancet/s0140673606694919.pdf

13. H. Zangana, "The Iraqi resistance only exists to end the occupation," *Guardian*, April 12 2007. Available at: http://www.guardian.co.uk/comment/story/0,,2054881,00.html

14. According to State Department polling results obtained by the *Washington Post*. A. R. Paley, "Most Iraqis Favor Immediate US Pullout, Polls Show," *Washington Post*, September 27 2006.

15. E. Colla, Review Essay of N. Shamma's "Le Lute de Bagdad," *Middle East Report*. Available at: http://www.merip.org/mer/mer215/215_colla.html

16. J. Maunder, "Iraqi poet Saadi Youssef on 'bullet censorship'," *Socialist Worker*, August 26 2006.

17. The Iraqi Artists Association said in November 2006 that nearly 80 percent of the singers during Saddam's era have fled the country and that at least 75 singers had been killed since the US-led invasion of Iraq in 2003.

18. Crisis Group Middle East Report No. 34, December 22 2004.

19. Maunder, *op.cit*.

20. The local performance tradition, *al-maqam al-iraqi*, represents an important secular repertory of many semi-improvisational compositions, linking classical and popular poetry, based on a sophisticated unwritten traditional theory. It is believed that the oldest extant repertory, transmitted orally, dates back at least four centuries, probably with some even earlier features. Because of its historical, conceptual and terminological flexibility, *maqam* also gives shape to local and regional practices. Historically, ethnic and religious minorities in Iraq and elsewhere (for example Kurds and Jews) utilized *maqam* in ways specific to their cultural

and musical needs. Available at: http://www.cacac.org/Arabic_Music_Theory.htm

21. G. Foley, "Iraqis Blame US for death toll in bombings," *Socialist Action*. Available at: http://www.geocities.com/mnsocialist/iraq5.html

22. K. Al Mosawy, "No to the occupation," *Al takwin*, 2005, p. 24 (Arabic).

23. Sakina is the daughter of Imam Hussein, and the niece of Abbas. Hussein and Abbas were the grandsons of the prophet Mohammed. The four-year-old Sakina was the favorite niece of Abbas, who she called for help on her father's martyrdom. The image combines an ancient chivalrous protection of women and children with martyrdom and, effectively, sainthood.

24. Abu Nuwwas' Street runs along the Tigris river in Baghdad, famous for its bars, cafés, and fish restaurants. Named after the famous Abbasid poet (756–814 AD) renowned for his poetry expressing joys of wine drinking , satire, and sexuality.

25. S. Assir, "Naseer Shamma: Guardian of Sound," *Al Ahram Weekly*. Available at: http://weekly.ahram.org.eg/2005/758/profile.htm

HANIF KUREISHI

Weddings and Beheadings

I have gathered the equipment together and now I am waiting for them to arrive. They will not be long; they never are.

You don't know me personally. My existence has never crossed your mind. But I would bet you've seen my work: it has been broadcast everywhere, on most of the news channels worldwide. Or at least parts of it have. You could find it on the internet, right now, if you really wanted to. If you could bear to look.

Not that you'd notice my style, my artistic signature or anything like that. I film beheadings, which are common in this war-broken city, my childhood home.

It was never my ambition, as a young man who loved cinema, to film such things. Nor was it my wish to do weddings, though there are less of those these days. Ditto graduations and parties. My friends and I have always wanted to make real films, with living actors and dialogue and jokes and music, as we began to do as students. Nothing like that is possible any more. Everyday we are aging, we feel shabby. The stories are there, waiting to be told; we're artists. But this stuff, the death work, it has taken over.

We were "recommended" for this employment, and we can't not do it; we can't say we're visiting relatives or working in the cutting room. They call us up with little

notice at odd hours, usually at night, and minutes later they
are outside with their guns. They put us in the car and cover
our heads. Because there's only one of us working at a time,
the thugs help with carrying the gear. But we have to do the
sound as well as the picture, and load the camera and work
out how to light the scene. I've asked to use an assistant, yet
they only offer their rough accomplices who know nothing,
who can't even wipe a lens without making a mess of it.

I know three other guys who do this work; we discuss it
among ourselves, but we'd never talk to anyone else or we'd
end up in front of the camera.

Until recently my closest friend filmed beheadings;
however, he's not a director, only a writer really. I
wouldn't say anything, but I wouldn't trust him with a
camera. He isn't too sure about the technical stuff, how to
set up the equipment, and then how to get the material
through the computer and on to the internet. It's a skill,
obviously.

He was the one who had the idea of getting calling cards
inscribed with "Weddings and Beheadings" inscribed on
them. If the power's on, we meet in his flat to watch movies
on video. When we part, he jokes, "Don't bury your head in
the sand, my friend. Don't go losing your head now. Chin
up!"

A couple of weeks ago he messed up badly. The cameras
are good quality, they're taken from foreign journalists, but
a bulb blew in the one light he was using, and he couldn't
replace it. By then they had brought the victim in. My friend
tried to tell the men, "It's too dark, it's not going to come
out and you can't do another take." But they were in a
hurry, he couldn't persuade them to wait, they were already
hacking through the neck and he was in such a panic he
fainted. Luckily the camera was running. It came out
underlit, of course – what did they expect? I liked it;

Lynchian, I called it, but they hit him around the head, and never used him again.

He was lucky. But I wonder if he's going mad. Secretly he kept copies of his beheadings and he plays around with them on his computer, cutting and recutting them, putting them to music, swing stuff, opera, jazz, comic songs. Perhaps it's the only freedom he has.

It might surprise you, but we do get paid; they always give us something "for the trouble." They even make jokes, "You'll get a prize for the next one. Don't you guys love prizes and statuettes and stuff?"

It's all hellish, the long drive there with the camera and tripod on your lap, the smell of the sack, the guns, and you worry that this time you might be the victim. Usually you're sick, and then you're in the building, in the room, setting up, and you hear things from other rooms that make you wonder if life on earth is a good idea.

I know you don't want too much detail, but it's serious work taking off someone's head if you're not a butcher; and these guys aren't qualified, they're just enthusiastic – it's what they like to do. To make the shot work, it helps to get a clear view of the victim's eyes just before they're covered. At the end the guys hold up the head streaming with blood and you might need to use some hand-held here, to catch everything. The shot must be framed carefully. It wouldn't be good if you missed something.

They cheer and fire off rounds while you're checking the tape and playing it back. Afterwards, they put the body in a bag and dump it somewhere, before they drive you to another place, where you transfer the material to the computer and send it out.

Often I wonder what this is doing to me. I think of war photographers, who, they say, use the lens to distance themselves from the reality of suffering and death. But those guys have elected to do that work, they believe in it. We are innocent.

One day I'd like to make a proper film, maybe beginning with a beheading, telling the story that leads up to it. It's the living I'm interested in, but the way things are going I'll be doing this for a while. Sometimes I wonder if I'm going to go mad, or whether even this escape is denied me.

I better go now. Someone is at the door.

JOE SACCO

Down! Up!

December 2004. On the Euphrates River, in Iraq's volatile Anbar province, on one of the top levels of the Haditha Dam, isolated from the reserve marines of the 1st Battalion of the 23rd Regiment, which is head-quartered here, two U.S.

servicemen are tasked with shaping a motley group from the Iraqi National Guard (I.N.G.) into the sort of self-motivated, competent soldiers that can—in the words of President George W. Bush—"stand up" so that we can "stand down."

DOWN! UP!

by Joe Sacco © 2006

And if anyone is going to help Iraqis save Iraq, it is Sgt. Tim Weaver, but they won't be saving anything, he'll tell you, until they get small unit formations into their skulls.

Unfortunately, this afternoon's quiz confirms that this lot can't tell its "skirmish left" from its "echelon right."

And that makes Sgt. Weaver one disgusted fifth-generation marine.

EVERY-ONE THAT MISSED ONE—

STAND UP!

Sgt. Weaver's prescription for one wrong answer is ten push ups.

DOWN! UP! DOWN! UP!

YOU JUST DID TEN FUCKING PUSH UPS AND YOU DIDN'T HAVE TO.

ALL RIGHT, WHO MISSED TWO?

YOU'RE DOING 20!

J. SACCO 8.06

Ahmed, the interpreter, translates, and—

ON YOUR FACE!

ON YOUR FACE!

DOWN! UP! DOWN! UP!

GET OFF YOUR KNEES!

Sgt. Weaver and his Navy colleague, Petty Officer 2nd Class Scott "Doc" Saba, have just three weeks to whip these guys into shape before they'll be expected to "accompany and assist" marines on patrol, and so the Iraqis had better learn a few basic commands—in English—'cause any mistake out there and a bunch of friendlies are gonna get killed.

THREE WRONG: 30 PUSH UPS

HE SAYS HIS STOMACH HURTS.

I DON'T CARE!

HEY!

GET YOUR DICK OFF THE GROUND!

WHY ARE YOU FUCKING THE GROUND?

FOUR WRONG: 40 PUSH UPS

Sgt. Weaver, 29, a heavy equipment service manager in his civilian life in Crosby, Texas, can't believe these guys. They'd gone over the formations "with little army men" again and again.

One hapless fellow can't get past his 20th push up so an even harder exercise is substituted.

Doc Saba, a 37-year-old paramedic from Plymouth, Massachusetts, demonstrates.

THEY'RE CALLED BUTTERFLY KICKS.

IF I CAN GET MY SIX-YEAR-OLD SON TO DO THEM—AND HE'S TINIER THAN YOU—YOU CAN DO THEM.

I DO THEM WHILE I'M TALKING TO MY WIFE OR SON OR WHILE I'M WATCHING T.V.

FOR THOSE OF YOU WHO ACED THE TEST, EXCELLENT JOB!

YOU HAVE TO PAY ATTENTION BECAUSE IF YOUR FIRE TEAM LEADER GETS KILLED IN COMBAT, YOU'RE GOING TO HAVE TO STEP UP AND TAKE OVER.

NEXT WEEK WE GET ON THE RIFLE RANGE.

YOU'VE GOT TO KNOW WHAT YOU'RE DOING OR SOLDIERS ARE GOING TO GET SHOT IN THE BACK.

While the men go over the answers to the quiz, Sgt. Weaver steps over to where I've been sitting taking notes.

SOME OF THEM ARE UNEDUCATED.

In fact, only five of the 14 can read and write.

THEY'RE BACKWOODS BOYS.

SOME OF THEM HAVE NO COMMON SENSE, NO COMPREHENSION SKILLS.

It's time to check the make-up test of the guardsman who cheated.

Oops!

He still got three wrong!

I TOLD YOU WE COULD DO IT THE EASY WAY AND LEARN, OR WE CAN DO IT THROUGH PAIN!

Sgt. Weaver orders the fellow into a stress position and tells him to hold it for ten minutes.

EVERY TIME YOU STAND OR TOUCH YOUR LEGS OR ANYTHING, WE'LL START THE TEN MINUTES AGAIN!

I'LL GET IN YOUR MIND!

Before too long, the guardsman squirms upright and drops his arms. He's made to start again. Minutes later he's babbling.

IF YOU WANT TO GO HOME TO MOMMA, I'LL CALL HER!

J. SACCO 7-06

Now it's Doc Saba's turn.

DON'T EVER WRITE ANSWERS ON YOUR HAND.

EVER.

THAT'S CHEATING.

CHEATING DISHONORS YOURSELF.

WHEN I SEE SGT. WEAVER, I FORGET EVERYTHING...

YOU NEED TO REMEMBER YOUR 'RIGHT' FROM YOUR 'LEFT.'

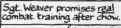

Sgt. Weaver, too, worries that they haven't got the basics down. He reviews hand signals they should know by now.

DIRECTION LEFT!

STOP FIRE!

ENEMY, 300 METERS!

They yell out the answers in English like happy school kids.

Sgt. Weaver promises real combat training after chow.

SO ALL OF YOU WHO ARE PISSED OFF AT ME, YOU CAN KICK MY ASS...

The Iraqis are given Meals Ready to Eat.

They pester Ahmed to translate what the packets and pouches contain.

THESE GUYS ARE IN MORE DANGER THAN WE ARE.

THERE'S MORE OF THEM GETTING KILLED OFF EVERY WEEK THAN AMERICANS AND COALITION FORCES.

WE GET THEM OUT OF THEIR ENVIRONMENT AND UP HERE 'CAUSE THERE'S NO TRIBAL CONNECTION AND THEY'LL BE ABLE TO FIGHT.

J. SACCO 7-06

In fact, none of these men, who were already in the I.N.G., knew they were in for this Marine boot camp stuff. One day they were locked in a room and the next they were in vehicles heading for Haditha Dam. For security reasons they were not told where they were going; their loved ones still do not know they are here.

The idea is eventually to reunite them with their families at some location far from their home villages, thus snapping their old loyalties.

After their three-week course, Doc Saba tells me, they'll have a graduation ceremony where awards will be given to the best and the most-improved trainee.

WE'RE GETTING A PATCH DESIGNED FOR THEM, SOMETHING TO BE PROUD OF.

WITHOUT THAT PATCH, AS FAR AS WE'RE CONCERNED, YOU'RE NOT AN I.N.G. SOLDIER.

Doc Saba, who was attached to the scout snipers, and Sgt. Weaver, who was pulled from the battalion's motor transport unit, put this program together in just two weeks.

I LOVE DOING THIS SHIT.

I LOVE YELLING AT PEOPLE.

After lunch, Sgt. Weaver demonstrates the "basic warrior stance."

STEP! PLACE! STEP! PLACE!

It's time for the Iraqis to try.

BACK! BACK! BACK!

FORWARD! FORWARD! FORWARD!

THIS IS NO JOKING MATTER. WE ARE TRAINING YOU FOR A REASON.

YOU JOINED ON YOUR OWN INTO THE I.N.G. I DIDN'T FORCE YOU TO JOIN.

BEING A SOLDIER IS NOT EASY WORK.

Meanwhile, one guy still hasn't come to his feet. He's complaining about his hips. Not even Sgt. Weaver can shout him off the ground.

Doc Saba listens to the guardsman, but Sgt. Weaver's not having any of it.

LOOK AT THAT GUY. HE SAYS HE'S 28 BUT HE LOOKS 40.

HE SIMPLY HAS NEVER EXERCISED IN HIS LIFE, THAT'S WHY HIS MUSCLES ARE ACHING.

WE HAVE TO TEAR DOWN THE RECRUITS IN ORDER TO BUILD THEM UP.

WE'RE NOT TRYING TO KILL YOU...

I AM.

The next morning, before sunrise, while the guardsmen are assembled on top of the dam to take showers in relays of four, I ask to speak to the trainee who has seemed the most serious about his instruction.

His name is Qaid; he is 24; and he speaks English.

Unlike most of the others, he is well schooled. He has a degree in mathematics from the educational college in Ramadi.

But teaching jobs are dependent on connections and corruption, he says, while—

—YOU CAN GO TO ANY I.N.G. CAMP...AND GET HIRED JUST LIKE THAT.

And even though the I.N.G. is targeted relentlessly by the insurgents, it offers Qaid one of the only steady sources of income available to him.

I AM A POOR MAN.

THERE ARE 14 PEOPLE IN MY FAMILY...

IT'S A HARD SITUATION IN GENERAL.

Qaid has other reasons for earning money any way he can.

I WAS IN LOVE WITH A WOMAN, BUT I COULDN'T MARRY HER BECAUSE I AM VERY POOR AND SHE IS FROM A HIGH CLASS FAMILY. I'LL DO ANYTHING IN THE WORLD TO MARRY HER.

But now he is having second thoughts about the I.N.G.

I DIDN'T KNOW I WAS COMING TO HADITHA.

I DON'T WANT TO STAY IN THE GUARD.

FIRST THING, I LIKE THE CIVILIAN LIFE.

THE MILITARY LIFE NOW IN IRAQ IS UGLY.

THIRD, MOST OF THE OFFICERS ARE CORRUPT.

He says he intends to "quit" in a couple of months.

I HOPE IN THE FUTURE TO HAVE A SCHOLARSHIP TO GET TO ANY OTHER COUNTRY IN THE WORLD.

AND I WILL TRY TO GET ANOTHER CITIZENSHIP...

THEN I WILL BE HAPPY — BECAUSE I AM FINISHED WITH IRAQ.

RUN IN AND TELL OMER, IF HE CAN'T GET OUT OF THE SHOWER NOW, I'M GONNA CUT HIS DICK OFF!

I KNOW ARABIC, TOO:

'GET THE FUCK OVER HERE!'

THEY SEEM TO KNOW WHAT THAT MEANS.

J. SACCO 8-06

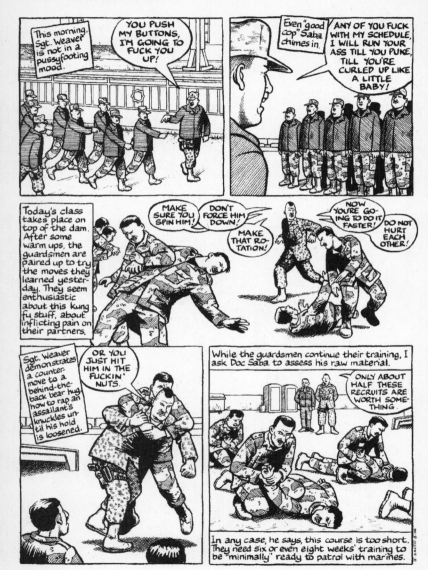

J. SACCO 8-06

He thinks only five of the guardsmen are worth his time.

THE REST OF THEM, THEY ARE KIDS.

THEY ARE NOT MEN.

THE ONES THAT ARE MEN, THEY ARE RETARDED.

Today's lesson sputters to an end, and it's time for a pep talk.

WHEN THE FUCKIN' MUJ JUMPS IN YOUR FACE, YOU'LL START PISSING AND SHITTING YOUR PANTS!

INSTEAD OF BEING AN I.N.G. SOLDIER, YOU'LL GO HOME TO MOMMA AND PUT HER TITTIE IN YOUR MOUTH AND START SUCKING!

IF I WAS YOU, I'D TAKE THAT TITTIE OUT OF MY MOUTH...

GROW THE HELL UP...

AND GET THE JOB DONE!

Doc Saba lets them know about a group of Iraqi police just executed in Tikrit.

THE MUJ PULLED 12 POLICE OUT OF THEIR POLICE STATION... THEY'RE ALL DEAD.

AFTER THEY'D DONE KILLING THE POLICE OFFICERS, THEY THREW A SATCHEL CHARGE IN THE POLICE STATION AND BLEW IT UP.

THE MUJAHADEEN DON'T GIVE A SHIT ABOUT YOU.

WE'RE TRYING TO TEACH YOU THE TRAINING SO YOU CAN STAY ALIVE.

THE MUJ ARE REAL.

THE BULLETS ARE REAL.

AND IF YOU GET KILLED, THAT'S REAL.

He tells them they'll be expected to encourage others to join the I.N.G. Then:

PRESIDENT BUSH WANTS TO SEE YOUR COUNTRY SUCCEED.

PRESIDENT BUSH HAS HELPED YOUR COUNTRY A LOT...

DON'T LET HIM DOWN.

I DON'T THINK THEY GRASP WHY THEY'RE HERE.

After the session breaks up, I have a word with Ahmed, the translator, in the guardsmen's quarters. He has echoed Sgt. Weaver's commands all day, yell for yell.

He tells me about another translator, a friend of his, who recently was killed by insurgents.

THEY MUTILATED HIM AND LEFT HIM WITH HIS I.D. AND HIS PAYCHECK.

HE WAS WITH A MALE AND A FEMALE INTERPRETER, ALSO KILLED.

AFTER I HEARD ABOUT THEM, I WAS SHOCKED.

MY FAMILY IS PUTTING PRESSURE ON ME TO STOP THIS WORK.

BUT I'D WORK FOR FREE.

I WANT THESE PEOPLE TO GET ON THEIR FEET...

IF THEY DIE, THEY EACH BETTER KILL ONE OF THE INSURGENTS.

ALL THESE GUYS WANT TO QUIT.

THEY DON'T WANT TO DO THE HARD WORK.

THEY'RE ALL THINKING THAT THE AMERICANS GET PISSED OFF AND HAVE COME TO CHEW THEIR ASSES.

AMERICANS WANT THEM TO BE STRONG.

J. SACCO 8-06

I spend a little time with a few guardsmen who are willing to talk to me.

They all seem to come from big families.

Most were out of work or under-employed when they joined the I.N.G., which pays a few hundred dollars per month—good money here.

They say they are proud to be guardsmen...

that they want to fight the insurgents...

and that they think the training they're undergoing is good.

I wonder if they are telling me what they think I want to hear. I wonder if they think I am going to report what they say to Sgt. Weaver or Petty Officer Second Class Saba.

I search out Qaid, who seems to have few reservations about speaking his mind.

THESE MARTIAL ARTS ARE NOT EFFECTIVE BECAUSE YOU CAN'T RESIST THE MUJAHADEEN WITH YOUR HANDS.

THE MUJAHADEEN COME TO YOU ARMED, THEY'LL SURROUND YOU, TAKE YOU TO AN AREA WHERE THERE ARE NO PEOPLE, AND KILL YOU.

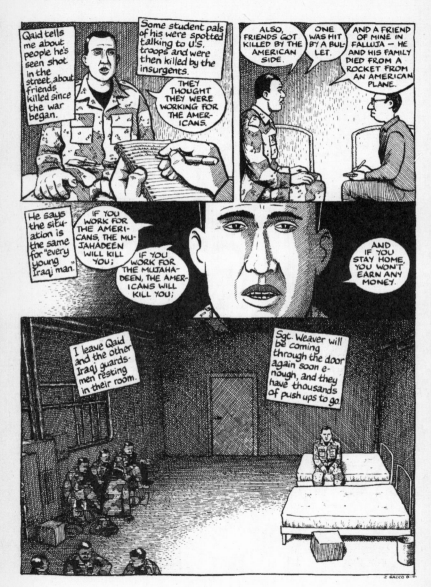

AHDAF SOUEIF

Mezzaterra

Holland Park. He came towards me through the crowd in the drawing room of the grand house that I'd never been in before and have never been in since. "Come," he said, "I'll show you the menagerie." That was twenty-five years ago. I have, in some sense, been examining the menagerie ever since.

I had thought it made no difference where one lived: Cairo, London, what was a four and a half hour flight? We were citizens of the world and the world was fast becoming more connected. I saw the difficulty only in terms of the personal life: on the one hand, how much would I miss my family, my friends, the sun, the food, the – life? On the other, what was life worth without this miraculous new love?

We married in 1981. But I did not move to London permanently until 1984 when our first child was born.

I shared, of course, in the general life of the country that had become my other home. I supported Spurs football club, kept an eye on house prices, formed political opinions and found that whatever view I might hold about Thatcher or Europe or the NHS, I was bound to find it expressed somewhere in the common discourse of the mainstream media. Where I felt myself out of step was when this discourse had anything to do with Egypt, the Arabs, or Islam. I had become used to what was at the time an unequivocal support for Israel in the British media, but it troubled me that in almost every book, article, film, TV or radio program that claimed to be about the part of the world that I came from I could never recognize myself or anyone I knew. I was constantly coming face to face with distortions of my reality.

I reasoned that this must be the experience of every "alien" everywhere and that it shouldn't be taken personally. But it was a constant irritant – and world geopolitics meant that interest in "where I came from" was growing. Lebanon was suffering the tail end of both the Israeli invasion and its own civil war (which was the direct result of the troubles in Palestine). Afghanistan became the crucible in which thousands of disaffected, young – mainly Arab – Muslim men were being transformed into a fighting force pitted against the USSR. Then the Soviet Union imploded. The Gulf War came and with it the imposition of sanctions on Iraq, the basing of US troops in the Arabian Peninsula and talk of a New World Order. In the run up to the Gulf War Israelis and Palestinians were summoned to negotiations in Spain and Norway and the world applauded while a perceptive few foresaw the mess for which the Oslo Accords laid the ground plan.

It was impossible – apart from a few notable exceptions – to find in the media of the West coherent interpretations of all this that did justice to the people of the region and their history. If the New World Order was a mechanism to control the Arab and the Muslim worlds then I felt that the media of the West was complicit in it; for they always represented those worlds in terms that excused or even invited the imposition of control.

Was this misrepresentation reciprocal? If I were an American or British person living in Egypt, and if I knew Arabic well enough to read the mainstream Arabic press, would I constantly be brought up short by skewed accounts of my history and culture? Would I switch on the television to find

a doom-laden voice intoning about how the Celts wor-
shipped the massive stones placed on Salisbury Plain by
astral beings? Would I switch on my car radio and hear an
account of yet another outbreak of "Christian Paedophilia"
with a background theme of church bells and Christmas
carols? Would I wander into the movies and come face to
face with an evil American character bent on destroying the
("third") world so the cinema audience cheers when the
Arab hero kills him? I have to say the answer is a resound-
ing "No." Where the Arab media is interested in the West it
tends to focus on what the West is producing today:
policies, technology and art, for example – particularly
as those connect to the Arab world. The Arab media has
complete access to English and other European languages
and to the world's news agencies. Where interpretative or
analytic essays are concerned they are mostly by writers
who read the European and American press and have
experience of the West. The informed Arab public does
not view the West as one monolithic unit; it is aware of
dissent, of the fact that people often do not agree with
policy, of the role of the judiciary. Above all, an Arab
assumes that a Westerner is, at heart, very much like her –
or him. Many times I have heard Palestinian village women,
speaking of the Israeli soldiers who torment them, ask
"Does his mother know he's doing this?"

Living in London, I know that I am not alone in the
experience of alienation; there are hundreds of thousands of
us: people with an Arab or a Muslim background living in
the West and doing daily double-takes when faced with
their reflection in a western mirror.

I went to school in London briefly when I was 13. Mayfield
Comprehensive in Putney. There, the white girls thought I was
white (or thought I was close enough to white to want to be

thought of as white) and the black girls thought I was black (or close enough to black to make identifying with the whites suspect). But that did not mean I could associate freely where I chose; it meant that I had to make a choice and stick with it. And whichever group I opted for I would be despised by the other. After three months I refused to go to school. Thinking about it now, I see this as my first serious exposure to the "with us or against us" mentality; the mentality that forces you to self-identify as one thing despite your certain knowledge that you are a bit of this and a bit of that.

Growing up Egyptian in the Sixties meant growing up Muslim/Christian/Egyptian/Arab/African/Mediterranean/ Non-aligned/Socialist but happy with "Patriotic Capitalism." On top of that, if you were urban/professional the chances were that you spoke English and/or French and danced to the Stones as readily as to Abd el-Halim. In Cairo on any one night you could go see an Arabic, English, French, Italian, or Russian film. One week the Russian *Hamlet* was playing at Cinema Odeon, Christopher Plummer's *Hamlet* at Cinema Qasr el-Nil and Karam Mutawi's *Hamlet* at the Egyptian National Theatre. We were modern and experimental. We believed in Art and Science. We cared passionately for Freedom and Social Justice. We saw ourselves as occupying a ground common to both Arab and Western culture; Russian culture was in there too, and Indian, and a lot of South America. The question of identity as something that needed to be defined and defended did not occupy us. We were not looking inward at ourselves but outward at the world. We knew who we were. Or thought we did. In fact I never came across the Arabic word for identity, *huwiyyah*, until long after I was no longer living full-time in Egypt. Looking back, I imagine our Sixties identity as a spacious meeting point, a common ground with avenues into the rich hinterlands of many traditions:

EGYPTIAN
rich tradition – cosmopolitan – old – modern – tolerant – inclusive – art source

ARAB
rich tradition – amazing language – common culture – oil – will be united sooner or later

AFRICAN
liberation – Black Pride – rich history – vibrant culture – the giant awakens

MUSLIM
benign – rich traditions and rituals – spiritual under-pinning – inclusive – humanist values – social justice – social cohesion – art source

CHRISTIAN
rich tradition – art source – historical intertwining

MEDITERRANEAN
rich tradition – art source – historical intertwining

THE WEST
culture and art – freedom – humanist values – pop & rock – fashion

SOCIALIST
social justice – equality – fairness – community – Che

NON-ALIGNED
pride – liberation – independence – development – strength – best of both worlds

PATRIOTIC CAPITALISM
individual – enterprising – reasonably well off

This territory, this ground valued precisely for being a meeting-point for many cultures and traditions – let's call it "Mezzaterra" – was not invented or discovered by my generation. But we were the first to be born into it, to inhabit it as of right. It was a territory imagined, created even, by Arab thinkers and reformers starting in the middle of the nineteenth century when Muhammad Ali Pasha of Egypt first sent students to the West and they came back inspired by the best of what they saw on offer. Generations of Arabs protected it through the dark time of colonialism. A few Westerners inhabited it too: Lucy Duff Gordon was one, Wilfred Scawen Blunt another. My parents' generation are still around to tell how they held on to their admiration for the thought and discipline of the West, its literature and music, while working for an end to the West's occupation of their lands. My mother, for example, who had fallen in love with the literature of Britain at school, and who could not be appointed English lecturer at Cairo University until the British had left, did not consider that rejecting British imperialism involved rejecting English literature. She might say that true appreciation and enjoyment of English literature is not possible unless you are free of British colonialism and can engage with the culture on an equal footing. This is the stance that Edward Said speaks of when he describes how "what distinguished the great liberationist cultural movements that stood against Western imperialism was that they wanted liberation within the same universe of discourse inhabited by Western culture."

They believed this was possible because they recognized an affinity between the best of Western and the best of Arab culture. Ideals of social justice, public service and equality, identified in modern times as "western," are to be found in the Quran and the traditions of the Prophet. If science flourishes in the West now, it had flourished in the Arab and Muslim lands from the tenth to the fourteenth centuries. The principles of objective scientific enquiry described by Roger Bacon in 1286 are the same as those expressed by al-Hasan ibn al-Haytham in 1020. Taxation and philanthropy produced free health care in Baghdad in the tenth century as they did in London in the twentieth. In both cultures a system of patronage had been the midwife to great architecture, literature, and music. And just as the European Renaissance had blossomed in the sixteenth century out of the mix of Europe's availing itself of Arab science while discovering its own classical heritage and enjoying an economic boom, so the Arabs looked to build their twentieth-century renaissance on their adoption of western science and the rediscovery of their own classical heritage. This was precisely the creative fusion behind, for example, the extraordinary innovative revival in Arabic poetry in the second half of the twentieth century.

Generations of Arab Mezzaterrans had, I guess, believed what Western culture said of itself: that its values were universalist, democratic, and humane. They believed that once you peeled off military and political dominance, the world so revealed would be one where everyone could engage freely in the exchange of ideas, art forms, and technologies. This was the world that my generation believed we had inherited: a fertile land; an area of overlap, where one culture shaded into the other, where echoes and reflections added depth and perspective, where differences were interesting rather than threatening because foregrounded against a backdrop of affinities.

The rewards of inhabiting the mezzaterra are enormous. At its best it endows each thing, at the same moment, with the shine of the new, the patina of the old; the language, the people, the landscape, the food of one culture constantly reflected off the other. This is not a process of comparison, not a "which is better than which" project, but rather at once a distillation and an enrichment of each thing, each idea. It means, for example, that you are both on the inside and the outside of language, that within each culture your stance cannot help but be both critical and empathetic.

But as the Eighties rolled into the Nineties the political direction the world was taking seemed to undermine every aspect of this identity. Our open and hospitable mezzaterra was under attack from all sides:

EGYPTIAN
disarray – corruption – weakness – disenfranchisement – economic and social problems – identified as enemy of West

ARAB
disarray – corruption – weakness – identified as enemy of West

AFRICAN
war – famine – Aids – corruption

MUSLIM
under attack – rise of extremism – identified as enemy of West

CHRISTIAN
Arabs subsumed in West *v*. Islam confrontation – discord with Muslim compatriots in Egypt encouraged by US – communities under Israeli attack in Palestine

MEDITERRANEAN
umbrella under which Arabs are forced to accept Israel without a solution to Palestinian question – anti-Arab and anti-Muslim sentiment growing in many countries – rise of right-wing white supremacist groups

THE WEST
revealed as still colonialist and racist – values discredited –
identified as enemy of Islam and Arabs

SOCIALIST
currently defeated

NON-ALIGNED
currently irrelevant

PATRIOTIC CAPITALISM
struggling – possibly on its way to extinction

Personally, I find the situation so grave that in the last six
years I have written hardly anything which does not have
direct bearing on it. The common ground, after all, is the
only home that I and those whom I love can inhabit.

As components of my Mezzaterra have hardened, as some
have sought to invade and grab territory and others have
thrown up barricades, I have seen my space shrink and felt the
ground beneath my feet tremble. Tectonic plates shift into
new positions and what was once an open and level plain
twists into a jagged, treacherous land. But in today's world a
separatist option does not exist; a version of this common
ground is where we all, finally, must live if we are to live at all.
And yet the loudest voices are the ones that deny its very
existence; that trumpet a "clash of civilizations."

Throughout the Nineties the world was treated to the
spectacle of the Iraqi people suffering under sanctions
because their dictator had invaded Kuwait, while next door
the democratically elected Labor government of Israel
speeded up its theft of Palestinian lands and resources under
cover of the Oslo Peace Accords. Neither process could
have taken place without the backing of the United States,
the world's one remaining superpower.

The effect was the radicalization of Arab opinion and the
exposure of the weakness and complicity of Arab rulers. In
the West public opinion was slowly starting to shift towards
a more balanced view of the Palestinian-Israeli issue. For a
brief moment at the end of the Clinton administration it
seemed that a solution both sides could live with was within
reach. It is said that Arafat was willing to accept the offer
Clinton put to him at Taba, but was advised to wait till after
the American elections. The reasoning ran: Clinton is on the
way out. He can't do any more good. George W. Bush is our
man; his Arab oil connections go back a generation. Let him
be the one to sign the peace between the Palestinians and the
Israelis. But before this could happen Sharon had gone for
his promenade through the Noble Sanctuary, the *Intifada*
had erupted, Barak was out and a Likud government was
in, and all deals were off. True to form the *Intifada* was
presented by most of the UK and the American media as
essentially a religious protest to Sharon entering the Haram.
Hardly any mention was made of the central fact of the
preceding seven years of collective Palestinian life: that the
Oslo Accords had been a new screen behind which Israel
could continue to dispossess the Palestinians. It was as
though a simple-mindedness descended on the media when
it reported on matters to do with Arabs, Islam and, particularly, Palestine. No, it's a bit deeper than that: it is that the
media attributes simple and immediate motivation to Arabs
and Muslims as though they were all one-celled creatures.
Watching the news on the BBC or CNN on the one hand,
and Al Jazeera on the other was like watching news from
two different planets.

As we now know, the New World Order announced at
the beginning of the Nineties was – by the beginning of the
new millennium – mutating into the Project for the New
American Century. An extreme strand of American ideol-

ogy deemed the omens propitious for America's "manifest destiny" to be actualized: it was time for America to dominate the world. The key to this would be strategic control of geography and of the main energy resource of the planet: oil. Dominance in Central Asia and the Arab world would both control the oil and prevent those parts of the world from forming alliances with China or Russia.

But the US could not underwrite Israeli policies and ambitions in the region and at the same time be regarded by the Arab people as a friend. The Palestinian issue was largely at the heart of this, but so was the Arab reading of Israel's desire to become the local superpower. Apart from the questions over the Syrian Golan Heights, the Lebanese Shab'a Farms and the never-quite-renounced expansionist "Eretz Israel" idea, Israel's footprint was to be found in many issues critical to the wellbeing of its neighbors, such as the debate over Egypt's share of Nile water, the surreptitious introduction of GM crops into the region's agriculture, or the growing drug trade. America, therefore, (and this is before September 11 2001) could not seek to secure its interests in the region through a positive or mutually beneficial relationship with the Arabs. Its strategy, certainly since 1967, was to support regimes which guarded US interests, regimes which then became more and more unpopular with their people.

This is never spelt out by the American media for the American public: that the discord between the Arab world and the USA is entirely to do with Israel. The International Court of Justice, environmental policies, globalization problems – these are issues between America and the entire world, not just the Arabs. Between America and the Arabs specifically there is only Israel – or there was until the US-led invasion of Iraq in 2003.

In the early months of 2001 the *Intifada* had unmasked the bankruptcy of the Oslo Accords, Israel was using increasingly violent measures against Palestinians and against Israeli Arabs, the people in Arab countries were agitating, collecting donations, and demanding action from their unwilling governments. In the face of the Palestinians' refusal to back down and accept their dispossession and with world public opinion shifting to support them, the US was essentially left with four choices. It could:

1. dissociate itself from Israel, or
2. pressure Israel into a true peace deal with the Palestinians, or
3. pressure Israel into disguising or deferring its ambitions and pressure the Palestinian leadership into conceding more ground to Israel, or
4. accept the hostility of the Arab world and a growing part of the rest of the world and decide how to deal with it.

The first option was clearly unrealistic. US domestic dynamics precluded it. Every American president, presidential candidate and secretary of state has felt obliged to swear an oath of allegiance to Israel in front of the powerful American Israeli Public Affairs Committee (AIPAC). The recruitment, in the late Nineties, of the Bible-Belt Right (now estimated to form 18 percent of total voters and 33 percent of Republican voters) to Israel's cause made it even more unlikely.

Yet an unquestioning pro-Israeli stance was becoming problematic as awareness of the plight of the Palestinian people increased in the US through the alternative media, the internet, and the activities of second-generation Arab Americans. The day might have come when American taxpayers realized that the billions of dollars they were paying to subsidize Israel were simply buying them the anger of the Arabs and the Muslims, and nudging them out of step with the rest of the world. They might have asked why this support continued to be necessary when Israel was the only nuclear power in the region, and had the fourth strongest army in the world, and was refusing to abide by international law even though it was no longer under an existential threat.

The second option was not possible for the same reasons as the first.

Options three and four have formed the basis of US strategy since 1967. Every American administration from 1967 to 2001 has tried to conclude interim peace deals which buy Israel time to create more facts on the ground. It is conceivable that had the events of September 11 not taken place, George W. Bush would have continued along this line. Being a declared non-interventionist and having big oil interests he might have pushed Israel harder and got something like the Taba proposals back on the table. After September 11 the total identification that has taken place between the US administration and the Likud government seems to preclude even that.

Since Richard Nixon's visit to Egypt in the early Seventies, American tactics for dealing with Arab hostility to US policies have consisted of increasing the region's (particularly Egypt's) dependency on the US through USAID projects, supporting corrupt Arab rulers and corrupting them further, advising and co-operating with regimes in silencing opposition, and attempting to co-opt local elites. Regimes that have balked at the American line have been branded "rogue" and sanctioned.

But with the escalating situation caused by the *Intifada* and the shift in world opinion in favor of the Palestinians something had to give.

The events of September 11 2001 played straight into what would appear to be the neocon dream scenario. With the collapse of the Soviet Union the US no longer needed the Islamist fighters it had helped to create in Afghanistan. In fact they had become a nuisance since the US refused to accede to the demand of its one-time ally, Osama bin Laden, that American troops be pulled out of Saudi Arabia. The political groundwork for dealing with the Arab world in terms of pure power had been laid by the neocons, who now held crucial positions in government. The ideological framework for a confrontation with "Islam" had been fashioned by Samuel Huntington and his followers out of the anti-Islamic discourse prevalent since Khomeini's revolution in Iran. Now the War On Terror was declared. Israeli politicians leapt to declare common cause with America, or rather to declare that their cause had always been the war on terror and now, at last, America had joined it.

It was now possible to move the conflict from the political into the metaphysical sphere: a conflict with an enemy so nebulous as to be found anywhere where resistance to American or Israeli policies might lurk.

It was within this rubric that the 2003 war on Iraq was started and it blazes on as I write. The old language of colonialism surfaces once again. Politicians and pundits insist on describing Iraqis in ethnic and religious terms although Iraqis describe themselves (in the Arabic media) in political and economic terms. The US insists on ramming a vicious form of global capitalism down Iraq's throat. In the western media Arabic is consistently mistranslated and mistranscribed and so leaves an archaic and inchoate impression. British and American heads are constantly to be seen on-screen discussing what "we" should do about Iraq, while coalition troops have until now killed an estimated 70,000 Iraqi civilians and 80 percent of the population of Iraq want them to leave their country.[1] Expert Western voices are raised every day against this adventure but leave no trace on events.

To date, the effect of American policies on the Arab world has been the complete opposite of their stated aims. In Palestine America defined itself as the "honest broker" between the Palestinians and Israelis, and proceeded to place matters in the hands of US Special Envoys, almost every one of whom was a graduate of AIPAC. Today, after more than thirty years of an American-sponsored "peace process," thousands of Palestinians and hundreds of Israelis have been murdered, Jerusalem is encircled by illegal settlements, the West Bank is decimated, an apartheid barrier is in the process of construction, and the President of the US has taken it upon himself to absolve Israel of any obligation to conform to past agreements, to international law, or to the declared will of the world. Gaza and Rafah are seeing killings and demolitions of homes on a scale unparalleled since 1948.

In Egypt, the late Anwar Sadat invited the US to set up its stall promising peace, democracy and prosperity, and the regime has toed the American line faithfully since then. The country now has unprecedented levels of poverty, huge disparities between rich and poor, and a shattered middle class. What small intimations of representative government there were have been strangled; Egyptians have been ruled by Emergency Law for the past twenty-six years and the abuse of the citizens' human rights has become endemic. So bad is the situation that Egyptians have reversed the trend dominant for some six thousand years and now seek to emigrate from their land.

Similar effects can be seen in every "third world" country that bought into American promises, or had them forced upon it. And still the media burble on about the "peace process" and bringing "democracy" to the Arabs. Almost 300 years ago, the Enlightenment philosopher Giambattista Vico pointed out that the first symptom of the barbarization of thought is the corruption of language. The media has a clear duty here: the US administration and the British government should be made to define very precisely what they mean by "sovereignty," "democracy," "freedom," "stability," "peace," and "terrorism." These people are not vague idealists; they are lawyers and businessmen, they know all about fine print. They run democratically elected governments answerable to the representative houses and to the people. The media should demand that they spell out the fine print in their pronouncements to their electorates. We could even limit the question and ask what do the British and the American governments mean by these terms in the context of their dealings with the Arab world? Then, depending on how the definitions agree with those in the Oxford English Dictionary, say, we could find different terms for the commodities Bush and Blair are so keen to export to the region.

And since the Western media is now blithely using Arabic words it would be useful if they could demonstrate their understanding of those too. They can start with *jihad*, *fatwa*, and *shaheed*, each of which is far more layered and subtle than you would guess if you just came across them in an English context.

The whole question of Islam and the West needs to be examined honestly. The current pieties that say "we know so little of each other" or, in the words of Lord Carey, the ex-Archbishop of Canterbury, "we must get rid of the deep hatred we have for each other," may be well-intentioned but they rest on untrue premises and are not helpful. The huge populations of Arab Christians and the Christians who live in Muslim countries know a great deal about Muslims and there is no evidence that they "hate" them. In fact Arab Christians have fought side by side with their Muslim compatriots against the Crusaders and against the Western colonialists of more recent times. And Muslims are very well informed about Christians. Eastern Christians have been their compatriots, neighbors, and friends for fourteen centuries. And Muslims have had to learn about Western Christians if only because the West has been the dominant power in Muslim lives for the last two hundred years. As for hatred, a "secular" Muslim cannot, by definition, hate a Christian on the grounds of religion. A "believing" Muslim cannot hate a Christian or a Jew because of who they are since Islam is clear that Muslims must live in fellowship with people of the Book. There is, though, an important difference between Christians and Muslims in terms of belief. Since Islam came after Christianity and Judaism and saw itself as a continuation of their traditions, it is part of the faith of a Muslim to believe in Christ, Moses, and the prophets of the Old and New Testaments. This is stated in the Quran and it is not open to choice. A believing Christian or Jew, on the other hand, can choose whether or not to believe that Muhammad was a prophet and, therefore, whether Islam too came from the God of Christianity and Judaism. This difference is well demonstrated in the language used by extremists on both sides which – while equally foul – differs in one respect: Christian extremists call Muslims idolators and regularly describe Islam and the Prophet in abusive terms. One high-level example is the Chief of US Military Intelligence, Lieutenant General William Boykin, who, while under investigation for boasting that "my god is bigger than his [a Muslim fighter's] god. My god is a real god, his god is an idol," is also being linked to the torture of detainees in Guantánamo and Iraq.[2] Islamist extremists at their most virulent never attack Christianity, Christ, or "the Christian God." They never speak against "Christians"; the term they use is "Crusader."

A linked and recurrent theme is to claim that Arabs use Israel and the West as an alibi, an excuse for their passivity; that they should get on with fixing their lives, with developing. Here it is essential to differentiate between the Arabs and their rulers. The rulers will do nothing because their only interest is to remain in power. They have failed in their primary task of protecting their nations' sovereignty and steering their countries' resources towards providing the people with a decent life. Their positions are now so precarious that they dare not move one way for fear that their people's anger will finally unseat them, and they dare not move the other way for fear of offending America. As for the people, they are doing plenty. First, they are surviving – by the skin of their teeth. The poor are poorer then they have ever been. The middle classes are often running two jobs just to make a living: civil servants are driving taxis, lawyers are working as car park attendants, graduates are working on food stalls. Even so, local NGOs challenge governments on human rights, on trade-union laws, on constitutional reforms. Citizens challenge government officers on corruption. They take cases to court and they win. Artists paint and musicians sing. Newspapers are full of analysis and debate. And this against a background of arbitrary detention, of torture, not just in prisons, but in police stations. Protests are organized despite the thousands of armed security forces the state puts on the streets. And despite the sullying of these terms, people still campaign for democracy and freedom.

What does the Western media report of all this? When British and American newspapers took up the case of Sa'd al-Din Ibrahim, the Egyptian academic with strong American ties who had fallen out with the government, you would have thought that all of Egypt was baying for his blood. No mention was made of the fact that Egyptian human rights lawyers across the political spectrum - including leftists unenthusiastic about certain of his American connections - volunteered to defend him. Similarly, in the ongoing case of the three young British Muslims accused (with twenty Egyptians) of belonging to the outlawed Hizb al-Tahrir, reports in British newspapers make no mention of the panel of Egyptian lawyers – again from right, left, and center – who are defending them. When the UNDP report on the Arab countries came out with its abysmal findings, where was the logical concern about the measly percentage of state budgets devoted to research and development and the trillions spent on importing western arms? Instead, the headlines screamed about how 50 percent of Arab women were still illiterate. Another finding was that in the last two decades Arab women outstripped every other group of women in the world in the advances they had made. Why was that not a headline?

It should be said that representation in the Western media is not high among the priorities of my friends in Egypt and other Arab countries. Nor should it be. But for those of us who live in the West this fashioning of an image that is so at variance with the truth is very troubling. As Jean Genet observed in *Un captif amoureux*, the mask of the image can be used to manipulate reality to sinister ends. And while it would not be correct to attribute malign motives to the media in general, it is not unreasonable to feel that by promoting a picture of the Arab world that is essentially passive, primitive, and hopeless, a picture that hardly ever depicts Arabs as agents of action (except for terrorists and suicide bombers), the media validates the politicians' dreams of domination. This, also, is where a certain breed of Arab intellectual plays a crucial role. Decrying the political oppression rampant in their countries of birth and exposing the atrocities that take place there, these intellectuals (the majority of whom are to be found in Washington DC) will implicitly widen their critique to discredit the very culture and people of these countries. They therefore provide the ideological justification to "save these people from themselves." This has been seen in action recently in the writings of Arab intellectuals embedded with the US administration encouraging it into its disastrous Iraqi adventure.

The long Editors' Note published by the *New York Times* in the May 26 2004 issue regarding its coverage of the Iraq affair, admits that "editors at several levels who should have been challenging reporters and pressing for more skepticism were perhaps too intent on rushing scoops into the paper . . . Articles based on dire claims about Iraq tended to get prominent display, while follow-up articles that called the original ones into question were sometimes buried." But the Note itself is published at the bottom of page A10 and, as Michael Massing points out in the June 24 2004 *New York Review of Books*, does not address the underlying causes of this failure. It is interesting that the bravest and most objective analyses of the events of the past four years have tended to come from the "cultural" rather than the "news" media.

It has become commonplace to say that the world has never known such dangerous times. It's possibly true. The givens we live with at the moment are well-rehearsed: the absence of a world power alternative to that of the United States, the US's umbilical links with the global ambitions of capital and corporatism, and the reach and power of contemporary weapons.

I would add to these that the identification (despite the efforts at blurring) of Islam as "the enemy" is particularly dangerous. When the West identified the USSR as "the enemy" it had to construct the "Evil Empire" from scratch.

But with Islam, the ideologues and propagandists of the West need only revive old colonialist and orientalist ideas of Islam as an inherently fanatical, violent ideological system that rejects modernity. They can play to deep-seated fears and prejudices with roots stretching back into the Middle Ages. When, at the height of the Troubles, the IRA launched a bombing campaign on the mainland, the suggestion that this was a manifestation of "Catholic fanaticism" was a marginal one. However repellent their bombing of civilians, it had to be regarded and dealt with as a politically motivated act. A similar reaction was afforded the African National Congress's bombing campaign – no reasonable person suggested that this was "black fanaticism." From 1970 to 2000 the United States has been directly implicated in creating and nurturing Islamist groups to counter secular national liberation movements in Palestine and other Arab countries. It, and the Arab regimes, have succeeded in pushing most political opposition into the cloak of Islamism. Now that the most militant of the Islamist extremists, whose lands are the "objects" of Western policies, are no longer content for the battles to be fought exclusively on their home ground and have brought a sample of the carnage into the territory of the West we hear a ready-made discourse on "nihilistic Islamic fanatics" who are on the rampage because they hate the democracy, freedom, and prosperity of the West. One does not have to condone the killing of civilians to admit the political demands behind it. In fact denying the existence of those political demands guarantees the continuation and escalation of the conflict and the deaths of yet more innocents.

The role of Israel here needs to be clearly acknowledged, for Israel has always predicated its value to the West on the premise that there is an unresolvable conflict between the West and the Muslim hordes. Today, allied to the American

Christian Right, its role is to exaggerate and escalate the conflict.

Imagine a new atrocity taking place in the US. General Tommy Franks has said that if that happens he can envisage the US being put under military law. All American dissidence will be suppressed; the administration will not even need to talk about democracy and freedom and beacons of light. And in response to America's deadly activities across the world will come a continuous asymmetrical terror.

Now imagine that this scenario is actually desired by the Christian Zionists who have allied themselves to Israel and who believe literally in Armageddon and cannot wait for "the Rapture," the moment when they, as good pious Christians, will be – in George Monbiot's phrase – "wafted out of their pyjamas" and seated at the right hand of God to watch what befalls us sinners. Among those people are some powerful officers of the American state, and they are interested in fomenting conflict, not resolving it. It sounds like science fiction but it isn't.

A bleak, bleak picture. And yet there is still hope. Hope lies in a unity of conscience between the people of the world for whom this phrase itself carries any meaning. We have seen this conscience in action in the demonstrations that swept the planet before the invasion of Iraq, in the anger of Americans and Europeans at the pictures coming out of Abu Ghraib prison, in the brave stand of the Israelis refusing to serve the Occupation and the private citizens from every part of the world who have tried – and some have paid with their lives – to stand between the Palestinians and their destruction. We see it every day in the writings of the brave and dogged few in the mainstream media and in the tireless work of the alternative and fringe media. It expresses itself in a myriad grass-roots movements that have coalesced into a world-wide effort to influence and modify the course of global capitalism.

For all these voices, these consciences, to be effective, however, Western democracies have to live up to their own values. It is shameful that on questions of international politics there is so little to choose between the governing parties and the opposition in the US and Britain. Democracy presupposes vigorous opposition on matters of national importance; it also presupposes a free and informed media who sees its task as informing the electorate of the facts. The current attacks on civil rights on both sides of the Atlantic, the drive to place security concerns before every other concern, the attempts to tamper with education and the law to serve a political agenda remind me of nothing so much as the activities of the ruling regimes in the Arab world for the last several decades; activities that have now brought the Arab world to what Arab intellectuals argue is the lowest point in its history.

The question of Palestine is of paramount importance not just because of humanitarian concerns about the plight of the Palestinians. It matters that, now, in full view of the world and in utter defiance of the mechanisms the international community has put into place to regulate disputes between nations, a favored state can commit vast illegal acts of brutality and be allowed to gain by them. If the world allows Israel to steal the West Bank and Jerusalem and to deny the history of the people it dispossessed in 1948 and 1967, then the world will have admitted it is a lawless place, and the world will suffer the consequences of this admission. The question of Palestine is also where the influence of the USA on world affairs comes into focus most sharply. If there is no just solution to the Palestinian problem, if the ordinary citizens of Palestine and Israel are not permitted the conditions which would allow them to live their daily lives in a human way, then the influence of the world's only superpower will be proved to be irredeemably malign.

Globalization is happening. It is driven by economics, economic ideology, and communications. But does this have to entail the economic, political, and cultural annexation of chunks of the world by whoever is the most powerful at any given moment? Surely that is the path to constant conflict, to grief and misery.

There is another way, and that is to inhabit and broaden the common ground. This is the ground where everybody is welcome, the ground we need to defend and to expand. It is to Mezzaterra that every responsible person on this planet now needs to migrate. And it is there that we need to make our stand.

NOTES

1. Iraq Body Count. Available at:
   http://www.iraqbodycount.org
2. "Rumsfeld defends general who commented on war and Satan," *CNN*, October 17 2003. Available at: http://www.cnn.com/2003/US/10/16/rumsfeld.boykin.ap/

TRAM NGUYEN

Homeland Wars

I met Elvira Arellano a year ago, in the fall of 2006, a few
months after she had taken sanctuary in a Chicago church. A
petite woman of 31, she had long brown hair tied in a
ponytail, and she was wearing sweatpants and flip-flops when
she greeted me upstairs in her small quarters at the church. She
looked young and even a bit hip, except for the careworn
expression in her eyes and the fact that she seldom smiled.

Arellano had entered the church on August 15 2006
instead of reporting to the Department of Homeland Security
for deportation as ordered. That summer, a storm of con-
troversy raged in the media and around the little storefront
church on, ironically enough, Division Street. An illegal
immigrant and a single-mother who had dared to defy the
law in such a public fashion, who claimed that she was
obeying a higher, moral law to provide for her child by
staying in this country where she had worked menial jobs
without papers for nine years – she touched a raw nerve in a
nation five years-deep into its post-9/11 immigration debate.

In the *Chicago Tribune*'s editorial pages, her situation
was likened to the abolition movement during the time of
the Fugitive Slave Act; she was accused of giving birth to her
son, seven-year-old Saul, as a ploy to gain citizenship and
epitomized a racist stereotype of Latinas crossing the border
to have "anchor babies" on US soil. In between those poles,
the mainstream middle was sympathetic to her plight but

questioned the appropriateness of her actions. Of course every mother wanted opportunities for her children, but what made Arellano deserving of special treatment? How could we as a nation turn a blind eye to lawbreakers, and how could Arellano demand "rights" when she had, unauthorized, jumped ahead of others waiting in line to come live in America?

Arellano left her village in Michoacan, Mexico in 1996 when she was 23. There were no jobs for her there, and she needed to support sick parents. Her father had muscular dystrophy, her mother suffered from diabetes. She knew lots of people, friends and cousins, who had gone north. Her grandfather had spent his youth working as a bracero in the 1930s before returning home for good. So she joined a group of pollos (chickens), what the *polleros* (chicken farmers, as the "guides" transporting immigrants are known) called migrants, and took a ride on a truck to the border. She crossed at Calexico east of San Diego and made her way to San Jose, where she had friends, and soon found work in a laundry washing clothes.

Arellano met another Mexican immigrant in those early years in the United States, after she'd moved up to Washington State in search of more work. They had a relationship, of which she says quietly now, "It didn't work out." But it did leave her with Saul, who was born in Washington and was a baby when she moved them both to Chicago. Arellano struggled as a single parent, often unable to afford babysitters so that she could work. Through another friend in the Pilsen neighborhood, a Latino enclave where she'd found a small apartment, Arellano got a job at O'Hare Airport. She used a fake social security number to apply and began work cleaning airplanes in 2000.

In October 2001, Operation Tarmac began as an airport security initiative in response to the September 11 attacks.

Tarmac was one of the first post-9/11 policies to target immigrant workers in the War On Terror. As the secret detentions post-9/11 were taking place, federal agents initiated arrests at airports across the country, starting with 29 Mexican workers in Denver detained late September 2001 for document fraud. By December, the airport sweeps had become a multi-agency undertaking that continued into 2002 and eventually jailed more than 1,000 mostly Latino airport workers.

Arellano and Saul were sleeping in their apartment when eight ICE [expand acronym on first usage] agents knocked on the door. "I woke him up because we had to go, and he looked at everyone who was in the room with their radios and guns, and he started to scream," she recalled. "Since he was panicking, I hugged him and told him to calm down and to not ask me questions please, and I hugged him very hard. I told him that they would take me and that he would stay with the babysitter."

Arellano was charged with document fraud in a federal court and sentenced to three years probation. Her criminal charges, along with a prior deportation order, culminated with final removal proceedings in 2006.

Targeted first as a security threat, Arellano then entered the deportation system as a criminal alien and eventually was sent the notice, known as a "bag and baggage" letter, that immigrants receive when they are ordered to report with a suitcase packed for deportation. "I thought, but why, I am not a criminal. I am not stealing, nor did I kill anyone. I didn't want to steal an airplane, you see," she said. "Why do they take the taxes and accept my manual labor for nine years, but cannot accept the fact that I have human rights?"

Arellano's case is especially illuminating because she stands at the crossroads of several major directions in policy and political debate over immigration in the age of terror. Though the spotlight was on the stereotypical terrorism suspect – a man with what is perceived to be a "Muslim or Arab" appearance – many more immigrants felt the impact of 9/11 on their lives, communities and workplaces, from Somalis to Mexicans and Cambodians.

As an undocumented worker at the beginning of the post-9/11 crackdown, Arellano was among the hundreds of thousands of immigrants who from the very beginning were already being affected by government campaigns such as the airport sweeps, the Social Security Administration sending "no-match" letters to employers who then used them to fire or intimidate workers, and the launching of the Absconder Apprehension Initiative to track and pursue more than 300,000 "fugitive aliens" with outstanding deportation orders.

In a period of just over three years, between late 2001 and 2004, many anti-immigration national security policies were introduced. They had Orwellian names like Operation Liberty Shield (requiring the detention of asylum seekers), the VICTORY Act (threatening to outlaw money-transfer systems used by immigrants to send remittances), and Operation Triple Strike (stepping up militarization of the Arizona border).

At its height, the post-9/11 crackdown resulted in more than 80,000 men from 25 countries registered by the National Security Entry-Exit Registration System (more than 13,000 of whom were placed into deportation proceedings as a result of voluntarily coming forward). Ethnic enclaves like the Pakistani community of Midwood, Brooklyn lost up to 20,000 people who fled to avoid special registration. Around the country, the FBI began knocking on doors and demanding "voluntary interviews" with up to 11,000 Arab, South Asian and

Muslim immigrants, which also resulted in arrests and detentions.

When the most shocking, seemingly most egregious period of "midnight knocks" began to abate in targeted communities, what little public awareness that had been generated about the civil liberties and human rights abuses of the domestic war on terror also receded. The new, ratcheted up national security state had become more normal, and largely invisible in everyday life, except for those whom it harmed.

Immigration lawyer Sin Yen Ling, who represented thousands of immigrants in New York throughout the crackdown, later reflected on the influence of that period and those policies: "Though still stuck in national security rhetoric, the impact of these initiatives are not September 11-related in the way you and I think they are – which is impacting South Asians, Arabs, Muslims. The way it's playing out, the language, rhetoric, and initiatives initially used against South Asians, Arabs, Muslims are being enforced against all immigrants."

Years before Abu Ghraib, wrote immigration lawyer Serena Hoy, there was the sexual humiliation and abuse of prisoners in a New Jersey county jail. There, in 1995, guards forced immigrant detainees to perform sexual acts, and to assume degrading positions while naked. Not long after the September 11 attacks, a detainee in New York City's Metropolitan Detention Center sent a letter describing how guards ordered him to take off his clothes for inspection before throwing him against a wall and beating him: "I was all naked and bleeding while this was happening."

Hoy described how the skyrocketing rate of detention and its concomitant abuses in a large, secretive and mostly unaccountable system had come about primarily as a result of two 1996 laws, the Antiterrorism and Effective Death Penalty Act and the Illegal Immigration Reform and Immigrant Responsibility Act. The laws mandated detention for anyone in deportation proceedings as a result of a criminal conviction (which was also vastly expanded to include a wide category of offenses). She noted that "Immigrants have been ordered deported for writing bad checks, selling $10 worth of marijuana, or pulling someone's hair during a fight at a party."

These policies resulted in a tripling of the number of immigrants detained in prisons between 1994 and 2001, to a daily average of 20,000 detainees held in custody at any given time. In 2006, the Department of Homeland Security arrested more than 1.6 million people, both undocumented and legal immigrants, 230,000 of whom were detained. Since the passage of the 1996 laws, more than 1.4 million people – many of them with family members in the US – have been deported.

The arrests, imprisonment, and eventual exile overwhelmingly affect people of color, immigrants from Africa, Latin America and Asia. Yet the discriminatory nature of immigration enforcement policies and practices has been entirely subsumed by the issue of legal status. Even though undocumented white Canadians or Irish presumably cross borders with impunity, little attention is paid to the racial subtext of criminalization policies toward immigrant communities.

Immigrants' lack of citizenship, plus their perceived criminality as a result of violating immigration laws or an expanded criminal code applied only to noncitizens, lead to what is seen as an acceptable, mandatory minimum punishment – often either indefinite detention or exile. The equal protection clause, and due process rights that are nominally guaranteed under the US Constitution – rights which have long been undermined for African Americans by racism and which provide a foundation for civil rights struggles – are not even formally required for immigrants whose cases are examined in the judicial system. Along with racial profiling in enforcement practices, the chipping away at judicial review in the immigration justice system contributes to the double jeopardy that immigrants face once they enter it.

"Many people are confused. They think I had a court hearing and that I did not show up to my hearing, and they say, 'Oh, if she had shown up to her court hearing then possibly the judge would have given her a chance to remain,'" Elvira Arellano said. "I did not have the opportunity – it was already my deportation . . . And this is unjust to me, because they never gave me the opportunity to go before a judge, never."

Like other poor and dark-skinned communities, immigrant enclaves are sites of heavy surveillance. During the post-9/11 crackdown, immigration agents and FBI routinely conducted sweeps at restaurants and apartment buildings in South Asian and Arab neighborhoods. Mosques were also monitored, and Muslim residents in suburbs of places such as Dallas and Chicago reported seeing agents writing down license plates of cars and sometimes even tailing cars to their homes. According to a congressional briefing leaked to the *New York Times*, in 2003 the FBI was ordered to count the number of mosques in its field divisions. The tally was being used to provide a benchmark for the number of investigations and intelligence warrants an office could be expected to produce.

As with the war on drugs, the domestic war on terror created what sociologists had identified as "moral panics." These manufactured crises were instrumental in building support for Richard Nixon's 1968 launch of a war on crime, and Ronald Reagan's further expansion of anti-crime and drug policies in the 1980s. Instead of the dangers of the black ghetto, and the propagated fear of its corrupting influence as a source of drugs for white youth, the war on terror tapped into the already simmering social anxiety over undocumented immigration, powerfully paired with 9/11's terrifying televised images. Bush's rhetoric about going after "evildoers" in the war abroad translated at home to talk about potential "fifth columns" – among ethnic communities, foreign students, and radical academics. In 2001, the American Council of Trustees and Alumni, co-founded by Lynne Cheney and Senator Joe Lieberman, issued a report identifying colleges and universities as a weak link in America's war on terror and listing more than 100 professors described as working against the interests of Western civilization.

The legal and social space of criminalization, then, had moved into alignment with the legal and social space of wartime, which clamped down on civil liberties and whipped up patriotic fervor against perceived enemies at home.

Domestic militarization, according to the geography scholar and prison activist Ruth Gilmore, is composed of industrialized surveillance, arrest, conviction and punishment. Speaking to ColorLines at the end of 1999, Gilmore described a transition taking place between the traditional "warfare-welfare" state that the US had been since the New Deal era, to a new state built on a foundation of prisons.

"The new State is shedding social welfare in favor of domestic militarization," she explained. "Programs that provide for people's welfare, protect the environment, or regulate corporate behavior have been delegitimized and jettisoned. There is a new consensus among the powers that be that focuses the domestic State on defense against enemies, both foreign and US-born. What's new is the scale of militarism being directed at people inside the US."

The post-9/11 national security state was the product of domestic militarization and it was as much, if not more, of a racialized state than had ever existed in the US.

"Mexican and other Latino immigrants are again being cast as the anonymous 'bad guys' as they run up against the political, physical, and psychic borders of the US immigration debate," observed journalist Roberto Lovato. "Within this language of global war, Latino gangs, like immigrants, connect the security dots from cities and neighborhoods like those in San Antonio or Miami to cities and neighborhoods in Latin America. The case of Jose Padilla, former gang member and alleged US al-Qaeda operative being held indefinitely without charges, may preview the great fusion of 'Latino' with 'terrorist threat.'"

As the policies of the post-9/11 crackdown became absorbed into standard procedure, we began to see a return to business as usual but with greatly expanded powers and resources. Emerging in late 2002 was the Department of Homeland Security, with almost two dozen federal agencies under its aegis and the budget to make $4.4 billion in grants for state and local governments to combat terrorism.

Actual terrorist convictions remained nearly nonexistent (to date only 12 people have been charged with terrorism, and the charges were sustained against only four, according to the Transactional Record Access Clearinghouse). But the march of repressive policies against immigrants continued, and the vast majority of those harmed were low-income laborers, families, people with petty or administrative violations and few means to protect themselves against the systems arrayed against them.

In May 2005, the REAL ID Act was passed. Tacked on as part of a huge appropriations bill for spending on the war on terror and tsunami relief, the act became law without hearings or public debate. It required that by 2008, all states must comply with federal requirements for identification documents – requiring proof of lawful status, data storage and collecting of biometric data. REAL ID helped crack down on the state-level efforts to get access to drivers' licenses for immigrants. It also made asylum applications much more difficult than they already were.

This was followed in December 2005 by the infamous House legislation, the "Border Protection, Antiterrorism, and Illegal Immigration Control Act," introduced by Representative James Sensenbrenner. The bill essentially made it a crime to be an undocumented immigrant, with felony charges, potential jail time and a ban from gaining future legal status or re-entry to the US. The Sensenbrenner bill was the policy culmination of a political climate characterized by relentless hatemongering among nativists, the growth of more than 800 racist groups from the Minutemen to KKK and white supremacist organizations under the banner of anti-immigration, and the popular framing of immigration as a drain on public resources and a conduit for potential terrorists.

But it had gone too far.

On March 25 2006, more than a million people poured into the streets of downtown Los Angeles. In Chicago, 500,000 people marched. Students, families and workers, Mexicans, Central Americans and also sizeable numbers of Asians and Africans in the Northeast, came out of the shadows boldly. They seized the attention of the nation, and electrified a movement that had been on the defensive for years.

The marches were a movement-building moment. To be

sure, they came in response to a direct attack, the clear threat and disrespect represented by the Sensenbrenner bill, and many complications and questions arose soon after – who were its leaders, what about the Mexican flags, what about the American flags waved, was there a coherent message or demand? Already, mainstream caution and conservative tendencies came to the fore, as pragmatic concerns took over about directing this grassroots mobilization into legal reform. Nevertheless, the marches were pivotal – a coming together of the political moment with the power of mass numbers of people acting in public to articulate a collective grievance and collective demand for dignity.

Roberto Lopez, an organizer with Centro Sin Fronteras in Chicago, put it this way: "To see half a million Mexicans on the streets with Mexican flags – that never would have been the strategy. But we discovered that public opinion went up over the roof, at 70 percent, when people came out and marched. Public opinion was on our side, as opposed to the last 20 years when we couldn't woo that middle-class, suburban voter. When people mobilize and say things the way they are, they defeated the Sensenbrenner bill because it was racist."

There was a price to pay for this demonstration of strength. That spring, starting in April, the Department of Homeland Security launched a new program called "Operation Return to Sender," a campaign targeting the interior with border enforcement strategies. The operation worked with local and state law enforcement to track down and arrest immigrants in violation of immigration laws. By fall, ICE had arrested more than 14,000 people, and deported nearly 5,000.

Toward the end of 2006 came a series of intensive raids carried out simultaneously in six cities. First a Swift pork plant in Tar Heel, North Carolina was shut down and hundreds of workers arrested. Then came Greeley, Colorado, along with meatpacking factories in Texas, Iowa, Nebraska, Utah and Minnesota. More than 1000 ICE agents were deployed in what authorities described as the largest workplace crackdown in history. ICE Assistant Secretary Julie Myers called the raids a major victory in "the war against illegal immigration."

The raids were especially brutal. Journalist Marc Cooper described the scene in Greeley: "Shortly after 7 am a half-dozen buses rolled up with a small fleet of government vans, which unloaded dozens of heavily armed federal agents backed by riot-clad police . . . Some of the frightened workers jumped into cattle pens . . . Those who tried to run were wrestled to the ground. Sworn statements by some workers allege that the ICE agents used chemical sprays to subdue those who didn't understand the orders barked at them in English."

Department of Homeland Security Secretary Michael Chertoff himself explained to the press that these raids were intended to put pressure on the nation to come up with a legal solution to immigration, namely a guestworker program.

In March 2007, this strategy bore fruit. New Bedford, Massachusetts was the site of the most infamous raid yet. More than 300 women working at a leather-goods factory were subdued by guns and dogs and rounded up by armed agents. Their children were left stranded at schools and daycares, with one infant taken to the emergency room as a result of dehydration. The national media sat up and took notice at what the *New York Times* called "the indecency of existing policies . . . becoming intolerable." Senator Edward Kennedy, the paper reported, was "infuriated after visiting a New Bedford church basement and hearing tales of separated families and sick children . . . [he] has given up on drafting a new immigration bill. He has decided instead to get Congress moving quickly . . ."

The first half of 2007 marked a historic opportunity. Despite the remarkable suffering that many immigrant communities continued to face, and the virulence of a small but vocal wing of rightists and nativists, the undeniably broken immigration system had forced lawmakers to the table. At stake were the lives of 12 million people already here, and the future of many more family members and foreign-born workers looking to come.

But this historic effort of comprehensive immigration reform was happening in the context of what Roberto Lovato called "the post-9/11 ascent of the national security state." He wrote:

> In this sense, the United States has started resembling another country, one whose nightmares shaped much of my thinking about peace and justice: wartime El Salvador. The denial of habeas corpus, the normalization and legitimization of torture (by Alberto Gonzalez, the son of immigrants) and the exponential growth of immigrant prisons and prisoners signal how immigrants have been lumped with alleged terrorists to provide the rationale for the Salvadorization of our political, penal and policing system. The government has violently raided homes and workplaces, sanctioned slave-like working conditions and denied historic and fundamental human rights. Migrants see and feel the slow, gradual dawn of a mutating American dream.

Driven by a clearly corporate agenda, along with restrictionist aims, the Senate Grand Bargain, as it was known, drove the debate toward an excruciating choice. For the millions of undocumented present in the country, it offered long and difficult hurdles – but nevertheless a path to legalization. For the rest, it called for the scrapping of family visas in favor of an elitist point system tilted toward rich, skilled applicants; an expanded guestworker system; and the requisite expansion of detention beds, border agents, and militarization.

The immigrant rights movement, and the mobilizations which had been key in bringing the nation to this point of problem-solving, had arrived at the corridors of power where tradeoffs, amendments and votes were negotiated in backroom deals. In the face of powerful interests and institutions, ordinary people had only what they have always had: faith in what they know is right, and love for their families.

Elvira Arellano, along with organizer Emma Lozano, released a profoundly clear statement in the midst of the political cacophony:

> We believed that the popular coalition, which mobilized the undocumented and the Latino community, was necessary to bring the legislative coalition to take and win the maximum gain in this current battle over reform of the law. We also recognized that the struggle does not stop with the passage of a new law, as the Black Liberation struggle did not stop with the passage of the civil rights act, but that the legislative coalition was necessary because our people wanted and needed immediate relief from the attack on their dignity and standard of living.

At the time of writing, Senate and House negotiations on immigration reform have only begun to move forward – a tenuous process that involves holding together a bipartisan coalition with polarized bases. But any legal reform gained will be a partial one, and immigrant leaders know that our short-term goal, as Arellano and Lozano wrote, is to "provide for the security, dignity and empowerment of millions of our people so that we can continue the struggle in the years to come."

Long before we come to the policymaking arena, there is a battle to define the terms of the debate. This is the terrain that the right has been so successful at seizing, points out veteran movement organizer Gary Delgado. "The buzz words that define how Americans think about pivotal issues in the civil and human rights arena are carefully crafted and publicly delivered by credible messengers, so that not only the end result but the very parameters of the discussion advance a conservative framework," he wrote in a paper entitled "Reclaiming Reframed Rights."

Pivotal events, clever language, and legitimizing messengers play key roles in refocusing the meaning of critical debates involving race, Delgado explained. As with the moral panics and fear of social disorder at the start of the war on drugs and crime, the domestic war on terror was launched under the extraordinary tragedy of September 11 and the then ongoing project of war abroad. Racialized enemies of national security expanded to include immigrants along with Muslims, whatever the practicality or rationality of declaring war on millions of ordinary people. Yet reframing the purpose of immigration policy from family reunification to upholding national security, as Delgado pointed out, paid crucial dividends for conservatives. They now hold the political advantage of having positioned the parameters of debate.

Along with the hard work of laying the groundwork for future organizing, rather than the de-mobilization of immigrant communities, our movement needs to take up this critical task of re-framing ideas and putting forth a new vision.

What would such a strategy encompass? Delgado lists some points for this agenda: push principles and values; pressure the Democrats to produce fair immigration policy; promote equitable racial outcomes; pummel national security policies.

Most of all, the key lesson to emerge from this period lies in our awareness that power needs to be built from the base, married with a sophisticated media and policy advocacy strategy. As Lovato writes, "Power cannot be built from the solely defensive position now defined for us by the national security frame."

A new sanctuary movement has begun, even as the spotlight has shifted from raids to guestworker schemes. The eighteen faith groups in ten states that have signed on to give sanctuary, along with the families facing deportation that have taken it, understand that whatever the outcome of the reform, immigrants will continue to be vulnerable to exploitation and punishment as long as the root causes of migration and poverty remain unaddressed.

From within the Adalberto United Methodist Church, the first person to take the risk that helped sparked a new sanctuary movement says she is at peace with her fate.

"I've learned so much, and I feel strong and peaceful," said Elvira Arellano. "I have faith that it will be possible for me to stay in this country and for all families to stay together."

SEPTEMBER 11TH FAMILIES
FOR PEACEFUL TOMORROWS

Not In Our Names

In the terrible hush that befell the world when the towers fell, all over the globe, in every nation, people and their leaders, stunned by the success of a few suicidal minds bent on murder, responded to our nation's loss with sympathy and compassion. We were not alone in our sorrow.

The greatest danger our nation faced at that moment was the danger of responding to hate with hate, of responding to the slaughter of innocents by slaughtering more innocents, the danger of ignoring the truth that the only way to triumph over hate and destruction is to not hate and to not destroy. An able leader, had we had one, could at that moment have demonstrated true greatness by resisting the deadly rush to retaliatory destruction.

But no. A handful of terrorists succeeded in their highest hopes. The chance for a peace never before known was aborted. People who placed their faith in the terror and awe of mass killing were in charge of al-Qaeda and the US government.

My son Stephen, 33, died in the destruction with so many others. I expect they had much in common, most of all their love of life and of their kin. What they also had in common was that strangers had decided they deserved to have their lives ended. Because of where they lived and worked, they had been determined to be the enemy who deserved to die.

In the immediate aftermath of September 11 my attention was focused on my family. Stephen's father, three sisters, four brothers, and I charted our collective and individual journeys through grief. But even before the veils of mourning began to lift, I spoke privately and publicly of my own certainty that a violent response was not the answer.

It wasn't until March 2002 that I found affirmation of my own convictions in a group known as September 11th Families for Peaceful Tomorrows, individuals who had lost family members and who had been brought together by Phyllis and Orlando Rodriguez's letter to the *New York Times*.

> Our son Greg is among the many missing from the World Trade Center attack. Since we first heard the news, we have shared moments of grief, comfort, hope, despair, fond memories with his wife, the two families, our friends and neighbors, his loving colleagues at Cantor Fitzgerald/ ESpeed, and all the grieving families that daily meet at the Pierre Hotel.
>
> We see our hurt and anger reflected among everybody we meet. We cannot pay attention to the daily flow of news about this disaster. But we read enough of the news to sense that our government is heading in the direction of violent revenge, with the prospect of sons, daughters, parents, friends in distant lands, dying, suffering, and nursing further grievances against us. It is not the way to go. It will not avenge our son's death. Not in our son's name.
>
> Our son died a victim of an inhuman ideology. Our actions should not serve the same purpose. Let us grieve. Let us reflect and pray. Let us think about a rational response that brings real peace and justice to our world. But let us not as a nation add to the inhumanity of our times.

My introduction to September 11th Families for Peaceful Tomorrows came by way of a statement on the Iraq War forwarded to me by a friend.

"The past is prophetic in that it asserts that wars are poor chisels for carving out peaceful tomorrows. One day we must come to see that peace is not merely a distant goal that we seek, but a means by which we arrive at that goal. We must pursue peaceful ends through peaceful means. How much longer must we play at deadly war games before we heed the plaintive pleas of the unnumbered dead and maimed of past wars?" Martin Luther King, Jr

September 11th Families for Peaceful Tomorrows condemns unconditionally the illegal, immoral, and unjustified US-led military action in Iraq. As family members of September 11th victims, we know how it feels to experience "shock and awe", and we do not want other innocent families to suffer the trauma and grief that we have endured. While we also condemn the brutality of Saddam Hussein's regime, it does not justify the brutality, death and destruction being visited upon Iraq and its citizens by our own government.

What others may view as a policy decision, we see clearly as the murder of innocent people. Death among the civilian population in Iraq will be immediate: the result of bombing that kills indiscriminately. Especially at risk are the children who make up 50% of Iraq's population. Death will also come later, from malnutrition and disease caused by the interruption of vital relief services and the destruction of infrastructure for supplying food and medicine. More deaths will occur years from now, as a result of the horrendous environmental impacts of waging war using lethal contaminants such as depleted uranium, a substance banned by the European Union.

We are also concerned about this war's consequences for America's military personnel, brave women and men who enlisted to defend our country, only to find themselves sent to fight an unjust war of aggression. Our prayers are with them and their families, and our hopes are that they will return soon.

Meanwhile, American citizens will bear the staggering costs of military action and the resulting reduction in spending on domestic infrastructure and social programs. We assert that Congress's lack of accountability for this war is a serious threat to our Democracy. We call on the House and the Senate to fulfill their Constitutional roles, both as representatives of the public will and as a check against the abuse of power by the Executive branch. And we call on them to defend America from all of the threats – economic, political, and military – that gather against it.

This war will not make America safer. On the contrary, it has already resulted in heightened anti-American sentiment around the world, and is likely to promote further terrorist attacks, not just today, but years from today. It will not protect American families from another September 11.

Therefore, members of September 11th Families for Peaceful Tomorrows will continue to oppose this war and to draw attention to its civilian victims. We will demand compensation for them, as we did for innocent civilians killed and injured by our bombs in Afghanistan. These casualties must be included as we tally the costs of choosing to wage war.

Finally, we will keep the faith with millions of people across the United States and around the world who have formed a truly international community favoring peace and declaring this war immoral. We are confident that, in spite of the events of today, the wisdom of their views will prevail as the 21st century unfolds, and as we continue to build a

global community that honors humanity, keeps families
whole, and renders war obsolete.

I had long before come to the certainty that, in relationships
between and among individuals and nations, violent retaliation only sowed more horror and more destruction.

In the mid-Sixties, when I had come to oppose the United
States' involvement in Vietnam, I became active in local
efforts to increase public awareness of the consequences of
this war, of the damage being done not only to the Vietna-
mese population, but also to our young people forced to
bear arms in a war that recognized no civilians. As a
member of Pax Christi, the Catholic international peace
organization founded by Germans and Belgians after the
First World War, I attended vigils, I pamphleted at defense
factories, I made long bus journeys to lobby elected officials
in Washington. And so, now, I reentered that way of
witnessing, standing in public places in candlelit vigils for
peace with local groups, traveling to participate in nearby
fasting and prayer observances.

Peaceful Tomorrows' statement against the Iraq invasion
brought me into contact with admirable people, refusing to
lapse into easy answers to hard questions. We recognize the
necessity to respond to violence and destruction, but at the
same time we proclaim that the lessons of history all lead to
one conclusion: non-violent resolutions of problems are the
only paths to lasting peace.

Barry Amundson, a founding member of September 11th
Families for Peaceful Tomorrows, speaking about the loss
of his brother, Craig, killed at his desk in the Pentagon,
declared in 2003:

There was an idea that 9/11 could be a "teachable
moment" – and that we had had enormous responsibility

thrust into our lives to make sure that our loved ones' names were not used for violence, but to teach peace.

Soon after 9/11, families started seeking each other out with similar views in order to provide solace, and organize. We formed Peaceful Tomorrows in order to put our "grief to work for peace as a path toward healing," seeking to highlight nonviolent responses to terrorism and to identify a commonality with all people affected by violence regardless of borders.

One of the first actions of members of Peaceful Tomorrows was to go to Afghanistan to share grief with civilian victims of the U.S. military action – to show the world that our experiences were not so different from theirs. This generated the first television news reports concerning Afghan civilian casualties. News editors did not have a way to present the story without seeming "un-American" in this time of fear. But because 9/11 families went they were able to have a sympathetic story about the Afghan people presented to the public.

Since then there have been other delegations to Afghanistan and then Iraq, lobbying and speaking out. That is what I believe the role of 9/11 families for peace is – to show the larger society and the world that those who have gone through violence and mourning want peace and reconciliation by standing with victims of violence. To respond to violence with nonviolence. Certainly it is the challenge of any victims of violence to overcome the simple desire for revenge and retaliation and speak out for reconciliation.

The same conviction that relying on military force is not only ineffective, but also counterproductive, because American foreign policy is the fundamental cause of terrorism, is expressed by Robin Theurkauf, another mother left widowed by the September 11 attack:

. . . while political scientists know very few things with any confidence, there is substantial consensus on at least one relevant point. While this attack was intended to provoke, responding in kind will only escalate the violence.

. . . Some have made the analogy to the attack on Pearl Harbor and in at least one way it is appropriate. In the aftermath of Pearl Harbor, thousands of young men volunteered to join the military. I can only imagine the success of radical Islam's recruiters after our bombs fall on their heads.

. . . In the long term, eradicating terrorism will require the elimination not of a group of people but rather of a set of ideas. Paradoxically, eliminating the people will reinforce and further legitimize the ideas. Terrorist impulses ferment in cultures of poverty, oppression and ignorance. The elimination of those conditions and the active promotion of a universal respect for human rights must become a national security priority.

Bombing Afghanistan today will not prevent tomorrow's tragedy. We must look beyond military options for long-term solutions.

When I have the privilege of speaking or writing as a representative of the members of Peaceful Tomorrows, I often recall the words of another founding member, David Portorti, who has carried the Peaceful Tomorrows' message to peace rallies in Japan and Korea:

While we know that the terrorist threat is real, I believe that we can pursue better, smarter remedies, using the power of alliances and the rule of international law.

. . . I believe that terrorism is not really the problem: terrorism is a symptom of the problem. The problem is militarism, imperialism, nationalism, materialism, the belief that the lives of some matter more than the lives of others. These are the problems and the misperceptions we must remedy, but we must first be willing to recognize them. And we must be careful to preserve our freedom in whatever we do. So much of what we are told today is that we have no choices – we must respond with force. But to me, freedom is about having choices . . . we must consider all of our options before choosing the last resort of war.

As I write today, June 16 2007, here are the headlines in the news reports:

Over 100 Killed in Southern Afghanistan (Associated Press)
More than 100 people – including civilians, police and Taliban militants – have been killed in massive fighting in the past three days in southern Afghanistan, Afghan officials said Monday.

US-led Airstrike Kills 7 Afghan Children (Associated Press)
Seven children were killed in a US-led coalition airstrike targeting suspected al-Qaida militants in eastern Afghanistan, a coalition statement said Monday. The strike came hours after the deadliest insurgent attack since the Taliban fell in 2001.

NATO Image Problem: Civilian Deaths (Associated Press)
NATO has an image problem in Afghanistan – and a US Humvee gunner who opened fire on a crowd of civilians following a deadly suicide attack Saturday shows why.

We must as a people accept the truth that our children, right now, are being ordered to kill in our names, and in the names of the gods of democracy and capitalism. Repeatedly we are told that our children must do bloody deeds and die bloody deaths in the lands of designated enemies, so that we do not have war in our own land. Surely such paltry, cowardly, unjust and merciless reasoning appalls every right-thinking person.

As a Christian, I follow a leader who explicitly instructed his followers to love God through their neighbors and their enemies. My country is led by an administration that claims to follow the same leader. Yet it impugns the faithfulness and patriotism of those such as myself and my dead son, and dedicates our nation's resources to killing those arbitrarily labeled enemies. Furthermore, the people now controlling our government have worked to implement an agenda that will result in securing riches for the minority to which they belong. This is being attempted, and yes, even accomplished by our leaders, not only in our own country, but in any country they declare to be an enemy and subject to their rule.

And this is happening in our day, in the very land to which so many of our forebears came, filled with the hope and trust to fulfill the vision of a nation dedicated to balanced cooperation rather than deadly attempts to kill [annihilate]problems. We as a people and as a nation have been guilty in the past of dreadful failures to live up to this ideal. In the evil consequences of such failures we have found the humility to pick ourselves up and start over again, to continue to seek new ways to realize the dream the founders began and we build on, to never stop believing we can keep striving for the ideals we proclaim to the world.

I am privileged to be numbered among the members of September 11th Families for Peaceful Tomorrows, and to have met, through them, the extraordinary individuals who were ripped from their lives and from our world. Through Rita, I met her brother Abe, who died with the wheelchair-bound co-worker he would not abandon. Through Colleen,

I got to know her brother Billy, who died because his work brought him to a one-day meeting in the North Tower. In Adele's home, I felt the presence of her son Timothy, and felt this valiant man's commitment to his duty as a fireman to save others. I know, through the writings of David, his brother Jim. I see in the eyes of Andrea, the deep reflection of her graceful geographer husband, a man who spent his lifetime embracing always deeper understandings of other cultures. These are the people whose gifts were taken from us that day, my Stephen with them. Stephen, who died in community, gathered in a conference room with co-workers sharing one working telephone to leave messages of love and caring, not of hate and revenge. When Stephen reached his brother Peter, and Peter implored him not to hang up, Stephen's gentle answer was, "I have to pass the phone on. I love you, brother. I love you, brother."

This is the legacy I work to keep alive – a legacy of love. There are hard days, when I go into a dark place, where the temptation to despair is strong. Coming out of that place demands determination, as we all know. My lifeline is the awareness that there are people who won't let go the belief that the earth is meant to be, and can be made, a good place for all people. The wisdom, the leadership, the commitment of peacemakers allows me, not only to persevere, but to work to persuade others that peace-making – not war-making – is the only path to justice, and to the peaceful tomorrows we all long for.

On September 11 2005, my family gathered on an island in Lake George in the beautiful Adirondacks, and on the fourth return of the day our Stephen died, we scattered the cremated remains so carefully collected and identified by the New York City Medical Examiner's office. As

Stephen's ashes floated away, mingled with the hydrangeas from the front garden of our home in Kinderhook, silent tears flowed as slowly as the waters, and three generations once more remembered our beloved son, brother, uncle, and once again admitted the grief we will never become used to.

NAOMI KLEIN

Building A Booming Economy Based on War With No End: The Lessons of Israel

On a single Friday in Spring, Gaza had fallen into the hands of Hamas, with masked militants sitting in the president's chair. The West Bank was on the edge of all-out crisis. Israeli army camps were being hastily assembled in the Golan Heights, ready for war with Syria. A spy satellite had just been launched over Iran. Another war with Hezbollah was a hair trigger away. And in Tel Aviv, a scandal-plagued political class was facing a total loss of public faith, with a president enjoying approval ratings of 2 percent.

At a glance, things were not going well for Israel. But here's a puzzle: why, in the midst of such chaos and carnage, was the Israeli economy booming like it was 1999, with a roaring stock market and growth rates nearing China's and India's?

New York Times columnist Thomas Friedman recently offered his theory. The Israeli education system and its broader society "nurtures and rewards individual imagination." That means that no matter what messes the politicians are making, Israeli citizens are constantly spawning ingenious high-tech start-ups that can sell their products and services across the "flat world." Friedman made this pronouncement after perusing class projects by students in engineering and computer science at Ben-Gurion University. Israel, he said, "had discovered oil." This oil, apparently, is located in the minds of Israel's "young innovators and venture capitalists," who are too busy making mega-deals with Google and Intel to be held back by politics.

But Friedman should have looked a little closer at the substance of those class projects at Ben-Gurion. It's no coincidence that they had names like "Innovative Covariance Matrix for Point Target Detection in Hyperspectral Images" and "Algorithms for Obstacle Detection and Avoidance." Those students were busy developing the latest weapons and surveillance systems for the Israeli state; thirty homeland security companies were launched in Israel in the first six months of 2007 alone.

So here's another theory: Israel's economy isn't booming despite the political chaos that devours the headlines. It is booming, in large part, precisely because of that chaos – because Israel, perhaps more than any other country, has learned how to build an economy based on never ending war. This phase of Israel's economic development dates back to the mid-Nineties, when Israel was in the vanguard of the information revolution. Thanks to innovations in communications, internet and medical technology, Israeli companies took the global economy by storm, with Tel Aviv and Haifa famously becoming Middle Eastern outposts of Silicon Valley. At the peak of the dot-com bubble, 15 percent of Israel's gross domestic product came from high tech and about half its exports. That made Israel's economy "the most tech-dependent in the world," according to *Business Week* – twice as dependent as that of the United States. Shlomo Ben-Ami, Israel's foreign minister under Ehud Barak, described the mid- to late-Nineties as "one of the most breathtaking eras of economic growth and opening up of markets in [Israel's] history."

Because of this dependence on a single sector, when the dot-com bubble burst in 2000, Israel's economy was left entirely unprotected. The country went into immediate free fall, and by June 2001, analysts were predicting that roughly three hundred high-tech Israeli firms would go bankrupt, with tens of thousands of layoffs. The Tel Aviv business newspaper *Globes* declared in a headline that 2002 was the "Worst Year for Israeli Economy Since 1953." And yet, somehow, by 2003, Israel was already making a stunning recovery, and by 2004 the country had seemed to pull off a miracle: after its calamitous crash, it was performing better than almost any Western economy.

What saved Israel's economy was the realization by its business and political leaders that 9/11 had opened up a new potential market niche for the country, as the world's leading supplying of "counter-terrorism" tools and services. The only reason Israel's post-crash recession was not even more devastating, was that the Israeli government quickly intervened with a powerful 10.7 percent increase in military spending, partially financed through cutbacks in social services. The government also actively encouraged the tech industry to branch out from information and communication technologies and into security and surveillance. In this period, the Israel Defense Forces played a role similar to a business incubator. Young Israeli soldiers experimented with network systems and surveillance devices while they fulfilled their mandatory military service, then turned their findings into business plans when they returned to civilian life. Like the students Friedman met at Ben-Gurion University, that's when the slew of new security start-ups were launched, specializing in everything from "search and nail" data mining, to surveillance cameras, to terrorist profiling.

Today, Israel has an estimated 350 companies dedicated to so-called homeland security – roughly equivalent to the number of companies that went bankrupt when the tech bubble burst. And no wonder: the super-growth that was once provided by the dot-coms is now coming straight from the boom in homeland security.

The timing for this switch was perfect. After September 11, followed by the bombings in Bali, Madrid and then London, governments around the world were suddenly desperate for terrorist-hunting tools, as well as for human intelligence know-how in the Arab world. Under the leadership of the Likud Party, the Israeli state billed itself as a showroom for the cutting-edge security state – a fortressed bubble where citizens enjoyed comfortable, western consumer lifestyles, despite being surrounded by people who wanted to blow them up. Israel's pitch to North America and Europe was straightforward: the War On Terror you are just embarking on is one we have been fighting since our birth. Let our high-tech firms and privatized spy companies – staffed by veterans of the feared Mossad and Shin Beit – show you how it's done. In short, Israel learned to turn endless war into a brand asset, selling its uprooting, occupation and containment of the Palestinian people as a half-century head start in the "Global War On Terror."

Overnight, Israel became, in the words of Forbes magazine, "the go-to country for antiterrorism technologies." Every year since 2002, the country has played host to at least half a dozen major homeland security conferences for lawmakers, police chiefs, sheriffs and CEOs from around the world, with their size and scope growing every year. As traditional tourism suffered in the face of security fears, this kind of official counter-terror tourism (along with visits from Christian end-timers) emerged to partially fill the gap.

During one such gathering in February 2006, billed as a "behind-the-scenes tour of [Israel's] struggle against terrorism," delegates from the FBI, Microsoft and Singapore's Mass Transit System (among others) travelled to some of

Israel's most popular tourism destinations: the Knesset, the Temple Mount, the Wailing Wall. At each location, the visitors examined and admired the fortress-style security systems to see what they could apply at home. In May 2007, Israel hosted the directors of several large US airports, who attended workshops on the types of aggressive passenger profiling and screening used at Ben-Gurion International Airport near Tel Aviv. Steven Grossman, head of aviation at the international airport in Oakland, California, explained that he was there because "the Israelis are legendary for their security." Some of the events are macabre and theatrical. At the International Homeland Security Conference 2006, for instance, the Israeli military staged an elaborate "simulation of a mass casualty disaster that started in the city of Ness Ziona and concluded in Asaf Harofeh Hospital," according to the organizers.

These are not policy conferences, but highly lucrative trade shows designed to demonstrate the prowess of Israeli security firms. As a result, Israel's technology sector, much of it linked to security, grew by 16 percent in 2006 alone and now makes up 60 per cent of all exports. Israel has more technology stocks listed on the Nasdaq exchange than any other foreign country and it has more tech patents registered in the US than China and India combined.

Then there are the weapons exports. Discussions of Israel's military trade usually focus on the flow of weapons into the country – US-made Caterpillar bulldozers used to destroy homes in the West Bank and British companies supplying parts for F-16s. Overlooked is Israel's huge and expanding export business. Israel now sends $1.2 billion in "defense" products to the United States – up dramatically from $270 million in 1999. In 2006 Israel exported $3.4 billion in defense products – well over a billion more than it received in US military

aid. That makes Israel the fourth-largest arms dealer in
the world, overtaking Britain.

Much of this growth has been in the so-called homeland
security sector. By the end of 2007, Israeli exports in the
sector will reach $1.2 billion – an increase of 20 percent in a
single year. The key products and services are the tools and
technologies Israel has used to lock-in the occupied territories.

Here is a small sampling of how Israel's firms have turned
the global obsession with security into a booming sub-
sector of the economy:

A call made to the New York Police Department will be
recorded and analyzed on technology created by Nice
Systems, an Israeli company. Nice also monitors communication for the LA Police and Time Warner, as well as
providing video surveillance cameras to Ronald Reagan
National Airport in Washington DC, among dozens of
other top clients.

Images captured in the London tube system are recorded
on Verint video surveillance cameras, owned by the Israeli
technology giant Comverse. Verint surveillance gear is also
used at the US Department of Defense, Washington's Dulles
International Airport, on Capitol Hill and the Montreal
Métro. The company has surveillance clients in more than
fifty countries and also helps corporate giants like Home
Depot and Target keep an eye on their workers.

Employees of the cities of Los Angeles and Columbus,
Ohio, carry electronic "smartcard" IDs made by the Israeli
company SuperCom, which boasts the former CIA director
James Woolsey as the chair of its advisory board. An
unnamed European country has gone with SuperCom for
a national ID program; another has commissioned a pilot
program for "biometric passports," both highly controver-
sial initiatives.

The firewalls in the computer networks of some of the largest electricity companies in the US were built by the Israeli tech giant Check Point, though the companies have chosen to keep their names secret. According to the company, "89% of Fortune 500 companies use Check Point security solutions" – a stunning number.

In the run-up to the 2007 Super Bowl, all the workers at the Miami International Airport received training to identify "bad people, not just bad things" using a psychological system called Behavior Pattern Recognition, developed by the Israeli firm New Age Security Solutions. The company's CEO is the former head of security at Israeli's Ben-Gurion Airport. Other airports that have contracted with New Age in recent years to train workers in passenger profiling include Boston, San Francisco, Glasgow, Athens and London Heathrow, as well as many others. Port workers in the conflict-ridden Niger Delta have received New Age training, as have employees at the Netherlands Ministry of Justice, guards for the Statue of Liberty and agents with the New York Police Department's Counter Terrorism Bureau.

The US Department of Homeland Security has launched a pilot project at an unnamed American airport where passengers are being screened using a new product developed by the Israeli company Suspect Detection Systems (SDS), founded by veterans of Israel's secret police. The new product is called Cogito1002, a white, sci-fi-looking security kiosk that asks air travelers to answer a series of computer-generated questions, tailored to their country of origin, while they hold their hand on a "biofeedback" sensor. The device reads the body's reactions to the questions and certain responses flag the passenger as "suspect." Not only has SDS tried out the biofeedback terminals at a West Bank checkpoint, it claims the "concept is supported and enhanced by knowledge acquired and assimilated from the analysis of thousands of case studies related to suicide bombers in Israel."

When the wealthy New Orleans neighborhood of Audubon Place decided it needed its own privatized police force after Hurricane Katrina, it hired the Israeli private security firm Instinctive Shooting International.

Agents with the Royal Canadian Mounted Police, Canada's federal police agency, have received training from International Security Instructors, a Virginia-based company that specializes in training law enforcement and soldiers. Advertising its "hard won Israeli experience," its instructors are "veterans of Israeli special task forces from . . . Israel Defense Force, Israel National Police Counter Terrorism units [and] General Security Services (GSS or Shin Beit)." The company's elite list of clients includes the FBI, the US Army, the US Marine Corps, the US Navy Seals, and London's Metropolitan Police Service.

In April 2007, special immigration agents with the US Department of Homeland Security, working along the Mexican border, went through an intensive eight-day training course put on by The Golan Group. The Golan Group was founded by ex-Israeli Special Forces officers and boasts over 3,500 employees in seven countries. "Essentially we put an Israeli security spin on our procedures," Thomas Pearson, the company's head of operations, explained of the training course, which covered everything from hand-to-hand combat to target practice to "getting really proactive with their SUV." The Golan Group, now based in Florida but still marketing its Israeli advantage, also produces x-ray machines, metal detectors and rifles. In addition to many governments and celebrities, its clients include: ExxonMobil, Shell, Texaco, Levi's, Sony, Citigroup and Pizza Hut.

When Buckingham Palace needed a new security system, it selected a design by Magal, one of two Israeli companies that have been most involved in building the Israeli "security barrier."

When Boeing begins building the planned $2.5 billion "virtual fences" on the US borders with Mexico and Canada – complete with electronic sensors, unmanned aircraft, surveillance cameras and 1,800 towers – one of its main partners will be Elbit. Elbit is the other Israeli firm most involved in building Israel's hugely controversial wall. Already Elbit's unnamed aerial vehicles, tested on bombing missions in Gaza and Lebanon, have been flown over the Arizona-Mexico border.

With more and more countries turning themselves into fortresses (walls and high-tech fences are going up on the border between India and Kashmir, Saudi Arabia and Iraq, Afghanistan and Pakistan), Elbit and Magal don't mind the relentless negative publicity that Israel's wall attracts around the world. In fact, they consider it free advertising. "People believe we are the only ones who have experience testing this equipment in real life," explains Magal CEO Jacob Even-Ezra. Elbit and Magal have seen their stock prices more than double since September 11, a standard performance for Israeli homeland security stocks. Verint – dubbed "the granddaddy of the video surveillance" – wasn't profitable at all before September 11, but between 2002 and 2006 its stock price has more than tripled, thanks to the surveillance boom.

Since Israel began its policy of sealing off the occupied territories with checkpoints and walls, human rights activists have often compared Gaza and the West Bank to open-air prisons. But in researching the explosion of Israel's homeland security sector, it strikes me that they are something else too: laboratories where the terrifying tools of our security states are being field-tested. Palestinians are no longer just targets; they are guinea pigs.

So in a way Friedman is right, Israel has struck oil. But the oil isn't the imagination of its clever young techies. The oil is the war on terror, the state of constant fear that creates a bottomless global demand for devices that watch, listen, contain and target "suspects." And fear, unlike oil, is the ultimate renewable resource.

The extraordinary performance of Israel's homeland security companies is well known to stock watchers, but it is rarely discussed as a factor in the politics of the region. It should be. It is not a coincidence that the Israeli state's decision to put "counter-terrorism" at the center of its export economy has coincided precisely with its unilateral abandonment of peace negotiations, as well as a clear strategy to reframe its conflict with the Palestinians not as a battle against a nationalist movement with specific goals for land and rights but rather as part of the global War On Terror – one against illogical, fanatical forces bent only on destruction.

Economics is by no means the primary motivator for the escalation in the Middle East since 2001. There is, of course, no shortage of fuel for violence on all sides. Yet within a context so weighted against peace, economics has, at certain points, been a countervailing force. In the early Nineties, it was Israel's business leaders – wanting to be part of the globalization juggernaut – who pushed reluctant political leaders into negotiations with Arafat. What the homeland security boom has done is to change the direction of that pressure, creating yet another powerful sector that is deeply invested in continued violence – and therefore threatened by the prospect of peace.

Now, rather than seeking stability in the interest of economic growth, Israeli businesses have been some of the noisiest cheerleaders for war. For instance, in the summer of 2006, when the Israeli government turned what should have been a prisoner exchange negotiation with Hezbollah into a full-scale war, Israel's largest corporations didn't just support the war, they sponsored it. Bank Leumi, Israel's newly privatized mega-bank, distributed bumper stickers with the slogans "We Will Be Victorious" and "We Are Strong," while, as the Israeli journalist and novelist Yitzhak Laor wrote at the time, "The current war is the first to become a branding opportunity for one of our largest mobile phone companies, which is using it to run a huge promotional campaign."

Israeli industry had no reason to fear the economic consequences of war. The Tel Aviv Stock Exchange went up in August 2006, the month of Israel's assault on Lebanon. In the final quarter of the year, which had also included the bloody escalation in the West Bank and Gaza following the election of Hamas, Israel's overall economy grew by a staggering 8 percent – more than triple the growth rate of the US economy in the same period. One month after the UN declared a ceasefire between Israel and Hezbollah, the New York Stock Exchange hosted a special conference on investing in Israel. More than two hundred Israeli firms attended, many of them in the homeland security sector. At that moment in Lebanon, economic activity was at a virtual standstill and roughly 140 factories – manufacturers of everything from pre-fab homes, to medical products, to milk – were clearing away the rubble after being hit by Israeli bombs and missiles. Israeli companies, however, were upbeat. "Israel is open for business – has always been open for business," announced Israel's ambassador to the United Nations, Dan Gillerman, welcoming delegates to the event.

Only a decade earlier, this kind of wartime exuberance would have been unimaginable. In 1993, Gillerman himself, then head of the Israeli Federation of Chambers of Commerce, had called for Israel to make peace so that it could become "the strategic, logistic and marketing center of the whole region like a Middle Eastern Singapore or Hong Kong." Now he was one of the most inflammatory of Israel's pro-war hawks, pushing for an even wider escalation. On CNN, Gillerman said that "while it may be politically incorrect and maybe even untrue to say that all Muslims are terrorists, it happens to be very true that nearly all terrorists are Muslim. So this is not just Israel's war. This is the world's war."

This recipe for endless, worldwide war is the same one that the Bush administration offered as a business prospectus to the military-industrial and nascent homeland security complex after September 11. It is not a war that can be won by any country, but winning is not the point. The point is to create "security" inside fortress states, bolstered by endless low-level conflict outside their walls. In Israel, this process is most advanced: an entire country has turned itself into a fortified gated community – a green-zone nation – surrounded by locked-out people living in permanently excluded red zones. What is happening in microcosm in Israel, however, is quickly spreading throughout the world.

For decades, the conventional wisdom was that generalized mayhem was a drain on the global economy. Individual shocks and crises could be harnessed as leverage to force open new markets, but after the initial shock had done its work, relative peace and stability were required for sustained economic growth. That was the accepted explanation for why the Nineties had been such prosperous years: with the Cold War over, economies were liberated to concentrate on trade and investment, and as countries became more enmeshed and interdependent, they were far less likely to bomb each other.

Yet at the 2007 World Economic Forum in Davos, Switzerland, political and corporate leaders were scratching their heads over a state of affairs that seemed to flout this conventional wisdom. It was being called the "Davos Dilemma," which the *Financial Times* columnist Martin Wolf described as "the contrast between the world's favourable economics and troublesome politics." As he put it, the economy had faced "a series of shocks: the stock market crash after 2000; the terrorist outrages of September 11, 2001; wars in Afghanistan and Iraq; friction over US policies; a jump in real oil prices to levels not seen since the 1970s; the cessation of negotiations in the Doha round [of WTO talks]; and the confrontation over Iran's nuclear ambitions" – and yet it found itself in "a golden period of broadly shared growth." Put bluntly, the world was going to hell, there was no stability in sight, and the global economy was roaring its approval. Soon after, former US Treasury Secretary Lawrence Summers described the "near complete disconnect" between politics and markets as "something out of Dickens, you talk to international relations experts and it's the worst of all times. Then you talk to potential investors and it's one of the best of all times."

This puzzling trend has also been observed through an economic indicator called "the guns-to-caviar index." The index tracks the sales of fighter jets (guns) and executive jets (caviar). For seventeen years, it consistently found that when fighter jets were selling briskly, sales of luxury executive jets went down and vice versa: when executive jet sales were on the rise, fighter jet sales dipped. Of course, a handful of war profiteers always managed to get rich from selling guns, but they were economically insignificant. It was a truism of the contemporary market that you couldn't have booming economic growth in the midst of violence and instability.

But as in Israel, that truism is no longer true. Since 2003, the year of the Iraq invasion, the index found that spending has been going up on both fighter jets and executive jets rapidly and simultaneously, which means that the world is becoming less peaceful while accumulating significantly more profit – a global version of the Israeli phenomenon. The galloping economic growth in China and India played a part in the increased demand for luxury items, but so did the expansion of the narrow military-industrial complex into what I call the "disaster capitalism complex." With so much of the apparatus of war-fighting, "peace keeping," reconstruction and disaster response contracted out to private players, global instability does not just benefit a small group of arms dealers; it generates huge profits for the high-tech security sector, for heavy construction, for private health care companies treating wounded soldiers, for the oil and gas sectors – and of course for defense contractors.

The scale of the revenues at stake is certainly enough to fuel an economic boom. Lockheed Martin received $25 billion of US taxpayer dollars in 2005 alone. The Democratic congressman Henry Waxman noted that the sum "exceeded the gross domestic product of 103 countries, including Iceland, Jordan, and Costa Rica . . . [and] was also larger than the combined budgets of the Department of Commerce, the Department of the Interior, the Small Business Administration, and the entire legislative branch of government."

Companies like Lockheed (whose stock price tripled between 2000 and 2005) are a large part of the reason why the US stock markets were saved from a prolonged crash following September 11. While conventional stock prices have underperformed, the Spade Defense Index, "a benchmark for defense, homeland security and aerospace stocks," went up every year from 2001 to 2006 by an average of 15 percent – seven and a half times the Standard & Poor's 500 average increase in that same period.

The Davos Dilemma is being further fuelled by the intensely profitable model of privatized reconstruction that was forged in Iraq. Reconstruction – even when it fails, which it so often seems to – is now such big business that every new destruction is greeted with the excitement of hot initial public stock offerings: $30 billion for Iraq reconstruction, $13 billion for tsunami reconstruction, $100 billion for New Orleans and the Gulf Coast, $7.6 billion for Lebanon. Heavy-construction stocks, which include the big engineering firms that land juicy no-bid contracts after wars and natural disasters, went up 180 percent between September 2001 and April 2007.

Terrorist attacks, which used to send the stock market spiralling downward, now receive a similarly upbeat market reception. After September 11 2001, the Dow Jones plummeted 685 points as soon as markets reopened. In sharp contrast, on July 7 2005, the day four bombs ripped through London's public transport system, killing dozens and injuring hundreds, the US stock market closed higher than it did the day before, with the Nasdaq up 7 points. The following August, on the day British law enforcement agencies arrested twenty-four suspects allegedly planning to blow up jetliners headed to the US, the Nasdaq closed 11.4 points higher, largely thanks to soaring homeland security stocks.

Then there are the outrageous fortunes of the oil sector – a $40 billion profit in 2006 for ExxonMobil alone, the largest profit ever recorded, and its colleagues at rival companies like Chevron were not far behind. Like those corporations linked to defense, heavy construction and homeland security, the oil sector's fortunes improve with every war, terrorist attack and Category 5 hurricane. In addition to reaping the short-term benefits of high prices linked to uncertainty in key oil-producing regions, the oil industry has consistently managed to turn disasters to its long-term advantage, whether by ensuring that a large portion of the reconstruction funds in Afghanistan went into the expensive road infrastructure for a new pipeline (while most other major reconstruction projects stalled), by drafting a controversial new oil law for Iraq while the country burned, or by piggybacking on Hurricane Katrina to plan the first new refineries in the United States since the Seventies. The oil and gas industry is so intimately entwined with the economy of disaster – both as root cause behind many disasters and as a beneficiary from them – that it deserves to be treated as an honorary adjunct of the disaster capitalism complex.

For the corporations that make up this sector, disaster is not a threat, it's a growth market – and many are doing everything they can to protect it. Large oil companies have bankrolled the climate-change-denial movement for years; ExxonMobil has spent an estimated $16 million on the crusade over the past decade. While this phenomenon is well known, the interplay between disaster contractors and elite opinion-makers is far less understood. Several influential Washington think tanks – including the National Institute for Public Policy and the Center for Security Policy – are heavily funded by weapons and homeland security contractors, which profit directly from these institutes' ceaseless portrayal of the world as a dark and menacing place, its troubles responsive only to force.

The homeland security sector is also becoming increasingly integrated with media corporations, a development with Orwellian implications. In 2004, the digital communications giant LexisNexis paid $775 million for Seisint, a data-mining company that works closely on surveillance with federal and state agencies. That same year, General Electric, which owns NBC, purchased InVision, the major producer of controversial high-tech bomb-detection devices used in airports and other public spaces. InVision received $15 billion in Homeland Security contracts between 2001 and 2006, more of such contracts than any other company.

The creeping integration of media companies with the disaster capitalism complex may prove to be a new kind of corporate synergy, one building on the vertical integration that became so popular in the Nineties. It certainly makes sound business sense. The more panicked our societies become, convinced that there are terrorists lurking in every mosque, the higher the news ratings soar, the more biometric IDs and liquid explosive-detection devices the complex sells, and the more high-tech fences it builds. If the dream of the open, borderless "small planet" was the ticket to profits in the Nineties, the nightmare of the menacing, fortressed Western continents, under siege from jihadists and illegal immigrants, plays the same role in the new millennium – not just for Israeli firms but for the sector as a whole. The only prospect that threatens the booming disaster economy on which so much wealth depends – from weapons to oil to engineering to surveillance to patented drugs – is the possibility of achieving some measure of climatic stability and geopolitical peace.

If we want to see where all this leads, we need only look to Israel. The fact that Israel continues to enjoy booming (if poorly shared) prosperity, even as it wages war against its neighbors and escalates the brutality in the occupied territories, demonstrates just how perilous it is to build an economy based on the premise of continual war and deepening disasters. This is what a society looks like when it has lost its economic incentive for peace and is heavily invested in fighting and profiting from an endless and unwinnable War On Terror. One part looks like Israel; the other part looks like Gaza.